ABOUT THE AUTHOR:

VANCE HAVNER became a preacher at 12, was ordained at 16, and has been traveling the highways and byways of our great nation for over fifty years, spreading the Gospel, bringing the Good Word to millions of seekers along the way, inspiring all with the *real* meaning of the Bible. Informally educated, Mr. Havner has been blessed with all the important knowledge a Christian needs, and has spent more than half a century helping others find the Way in these days of violence, self-indulgence and materialism. His many thousands of readers, and those fortunate to have heard him preach, will want to read this latest inspirational work, ALL THE DAYS.

All The Days

By Vance Havner

BY THE STILL WATERS
THE SECRET OF CHRISTIAN JOY
ROAD TO REVIVAL
IT IS TIME
HEARTS AFIRE
DAY BY DAY
REPENT OR ELSE
TRUTH FOR EACH DAY
PEACE IN THE VALLEY
WHY NOT JUST BE CHRISTIANS?
PEPPER 'N SALT
LIVING IN KINGDOM COME
JESUS ONLY
IN TIMES LIKE THESE
NOT PEACE BUT A SWORD
THREESCORE AND TEN
SONG AT TWILIGHT
THOUGH I WALK THROUGH THE VALLEY
ALL THE DAYS

All The Days

*Lo, I am with you alway [All the Days],
even unto the end of the world.   Matthew 28:20.*

VANCE HAVNER

Fleming H. Revell Company
Old Tappan, New Jersey

5007

Unless otherwise identified, all Scripture quotations in this volume are from the King James Version of the Bible.

Library of Congress Cataloging in Publication Data

Havner, Vance, 1901–
   All the days.

   1. Devotional calendars. I. Title.
BV4811.H295   242'.2   76–16281
ISBN 0–8007–0812–1

All The Days

JANUARY 1

EVERYTHING NEW!

Behold, I make all things new.   Revelation 21:5.

THE NEW YEAR should remind us of the greatest renovation project of time and eternity. The first Creation was wrecked by sin, but God began a new race with a new Adam and new creatures with a new life, a new name, a new song, a new commandment, a new heaven, and a new earth!

God is not running an antique shop! He is making all things new!

JANUARY 2

ALL THE DAYS

Lo, I am with you alway, even unto the end of the world.
Matthew 28:20.

ALWAY MEANS "all the days," any day, every day. There will be days when we are not conscious of God's presence, when it may seem that He has forgotten us, but He is there although we perceive Him not. Christ lives in the believer's heart and the Holy Spirit is alongside us to help. There are no exceptions—any day, every day, all the days— the promise holds. This day, today, is the day the Lord hath made. Let us be glad and rejoice in it. You may feel like saying, "This just isn't *my* day," but it is *His* day!

JANUARY 3

GREAT DAYS

Caught up into paradise. . . . 2 Corinthians 12:4. *When we were with him in the holy mount.* 2 Peter 1:18.

LIFE HAS ITS great days, supreme experiences—maybe when we were converted or made fresh contact with God, or when we climbed the utmost height and caught a gleam of glory bright. Maybe it was some outstanding event as when we were married, some outstanding achievement, some red-letter day. We could not live all the time in the rarified air of those dizzy peaks. We may have wanted to build three tabernacles to house those great days, but we must get down the mountain to live out among the cobblestones what we saw among the clouds. We thank God for the great days and He is with us in triumph as well as in trouble.

JANUARY 4

GOOD DAYS

Oh that I were as in months past. . . . Job 29:2.

JOB IS LONGING for days past when things went well before calamity descended upon him. The good days are not the rare and exciting great days but those times when heaven smiled upon us, when we had health and home and happiness. God was with us then and we need to recognize Him with special devotion for we are likely to take such days for granted. We never miss the water till the well goes dry. We had better let the goodness of God bring us to repentance for our unthankfulness. Make much of the good days while the sun shines and before the storm breaks.

JANUARY 5

DULL DAYS

Is there any taste in the white of an egg?   Job 6:6.

JOB COMPLAINS THAT he is reduced to egg white without salt. There are dull days when everything is dry, flat, insipid. No thought worth having comes to mind. The color goes out of living, the romance fades, a sense of things real comes doubly strong. Even black and white become gray. But God is with us on such days.

> We cannot kindle when we will
> The fire which in the heart resides,
> The spirit bloweth and is still;
> In mystery our soul abides.
> MATTHEW ARNOLD

But on such days, tasks in hours of insight willed can be in hours of gloom fulfilled. We can do a lot of chores until better hours return. Monotony wears down the spirit and may be harder to master than times of crisis. We can be bored to death! It just takes longer! But faith can serve God without feeling until better days return.

JANUARY 6

DARK DAYS

He hath set darkness in my paths.   Job 19:8.

THE SUN IS still there when we cannot see the sunshine. God has not departed because the day is dark. Sickness, sorrow, faded dreams, and broken hearts—how we long for the Land of Unclouded Day! But the brightest songs we sing hereafter may be born on the darkest day here. What we sob over now, we may shout about hereafter. God is with us though we see Him not. "The darkness hideth not from thee"

9

(Psalms 139:12). Darkness and light are alike to Him. We are on the underside, but by prayer and faith we can rise above the clouds, as we do sometimes in airplanes, to where the sun is shining.

JANUARY 7

EVIL DAYS

Deliver us from evil. . . .   Matthew 6:13.

EVIL DAYS ARE days of temptation when our guard may be down and our defenses are relaxed and the enemy comes in like a flood. Many a saint has yielded to the powers of darkness in his weakness and for the rest of his life has lived in self-condemnation and remorse. "How could I have done it?" is the constant wail of his heart. We are never safe until we get home. The bark may sink in the haven's mouth. So we must be watchful and alert, watching that we may pray and praying that we may watch, not tense and fearful but trusting Him who is with us even on evil days. He does not keep us from temptation, but He can keep us in temptation.

JANUARY 8

LONELY DAYS

He hath said, I will never leave thee, nor forsake thee.
Hebrews 13:5.

THE DISCIPLES FORSOOK our Lord, and no man stood with Paul at his trial. But the apostle adds, "Notwithstanding the Lord stood with me, and strengthened me . . ." (2 Timothy 4:17). There is no greater test than day-by-day loneliness when loved ones are no longer by our side and friends are busy with problems of their own. The long night when we long for the vanished hand and the sound of the voice that is still; the aloneness in the midst of a crowd which can be worse than solitude . . . there is no darker place in life's journey than Lonesome

Valley. But the Christian does not walk it alone. We must walk it *for* ourselves but not *by* ourselves. Jesus walked His Lonesome Valley for and by Himself that He might walk ours with us.

JANUARY 9

DESPERATE DAYS

Wilt thou be altogether unto me as a liar, and as waters that fail?
Jeremiah 15:18.

JEREMIAH WAS DESPERATE and even God seemed to have failed him. There come days when nothing makes sense, when the heavens are as brass, when Satan mocks our faith and demonic forces seem to wreak their havoc in unexplainable ways. Sometimes the saintliest souls end their days under a cloud, go out under the blackest of circumstances. You cannot make a uniform pattern from the death-bed experiences of Christians. The "others" of Hebrews 11:35–38 do not fare like their comrades in the preceding verses. In desperation, we leave the enigma in God's hands and press on to a brighter day when we no longer see as in a riddle.

JANUARY 10

DECLINING DAYS

And even to your old age I am he: and even to hoar hairs will I carry you. . . . Isaiah 46:4.

THE SENIOR CITIZEN past his threescore and ten is not left alone in the last phase of his journey. Much attention is paid to the aged today and politicians make many promises, but God is our mainstay and we do not pray in vain, "When I am old and grayheaded, O God, forsake me not . . ." (Psalms 71:18). These are the days, when, for the Christian, heaven draws nearer, when most of our dear ones have moved to the other side. The curtain between here and hereafter grows thinner as we await the parting of the veil. It is not the end but the beginning of a new day when we are promoted with the prospect that "his servants shall serve him."

JANUARY 11

THE LAST DAY

Yea, though I walk through the valley of the shadow of death, I will fear no evil: for thou art with me. . . . Psalms 23:4.

"ALL THE DAYS" includes the last day. It is well to "fore-fancy our deathbed" as one old saint put it, but not in fear for Christ has conquered him who has the power of death, and death, the last enemy of all, is headed for destruction. Death is not the end and our last illness is not unto death, but that God may be glorified as with Lazarus and as God told Peter. We must face it, but we need not fear it. It is the last of all the days and the last can be the best. It opens the door to a new succession of days that have no end.

JANUARY 12

IF HE HAD COME DOWN

Let him now come down from the cross, and we will believe him. Matthew 27:42.

So SAYS THE world today: Give us Christ without the cross. But a crossless Christ would mean no more than a Christless cross. We glory in the cross, but it is the cross that the world despises. It is the reproach and scandal of the cross that the world will not accept. "Save thyself," they shouted, but that was exactly what He could not do if He would save others. If He had come down, there would be no Saviour and no Gospel. Men will accept Him as teacher and example but not as the bearer of our sins in His body on the tree. The Paragon but not the Propitiation!

JANUARY 13

GOING UP TOGETHER

The dead in Christ shall rise first: Then we which are alive and
remain shall be caught up together with them . . . to meet the Lord
in the air: and so shall we ever be with the Lord.
1 Thessalonians 4:16, 17.

"TOGETHER WITH THEM!" That answers a lot of questions. "With the
Lord," that is enough said.

> With Christ! No more is told.
> What more, Lord, couldst Thou tell?
> That is enough to satisfy
> The heart that loves Thee well.

Astronauts sink into insignificance beside this Ascension! And on
our way up, who is so foolish as to fear that we shall not know fellow
travelers we loved long since and lost a while?

JANUARY 14

PURCHASING THE PRICELESS

He that hath no money; come ye, buy, and eat. . . .   Isaiah 55:1.
Buy of me gold tried in the fire. . . .   Revelation 3:18.

IF WE HAVE no money, how can we buy? How can paupers purchase
the priceless? God's grace is free, but not cheap. When we become
disciples, we become disciples and that will cost us everything. It is
the other side of the coin. We give ourselves, but we get Himself and
in Him we have everything. Some misinterpret free salvation to in-
volve no cost, no obligation on our part. Ours is the obligation of
repentance and surrender of all we are and have. But what an exchange for His gold and garments and spiritual vision—wealth, wardrobe, and wisdom!

JANUARY 15

WALK, NOT WALLOW

Though I walk through the valley of the shadow of death. . . .
Psalms 23:4.

A MINISTER, AFTER his wife's death, walked the floor night after night in an agony of self-accusation and regret. Finally there came to his heart this reminder, the voice of God saying, "I promised to walk with you *through* the Valley, not wallow with you in it. This is no time for bemoaning what might have been in self-condemnation that serves no good purpose."

Indeed, we ought to repent of mistakes made, confess any wrong, and claim cleansing, learn any needed lessons but walk through the valley, not wallow in it.

JANUARY 16

FELLOW TRAVELERS IN THE NIGHT

I call to remembrance my song in the night. . . . Psalms 77:6.

I PREFER SOME of the old tunes like "How Tedious and Tasteless the Hours," "O Thou in Whose Presence My Soul Takes Delight," and "Lead, Kindly Light" to the jingles of the modern Happiness Boys. "Abide With Me" may seem too melancholy, but the old-timers made their way "o'er moor and fen" and to them "the darkness deepens," "the encircling gloom," and "bid my anxious fears subside" grew out of grim reality. Blithe souls who have never known trouble have little to offer when the tempest rages and the floods descend. Then we turn to David and Jeremiah and Job and John, on Patmos, and our Saviour saying, "Now is my soul troubled and what shall I say?"

JANUARY 17

GOD'S "WHO'S WHO"

And Joseph also went up from Galilee. . . .   Luke 2:4.

AGAINST THE BACKGROUND of the mighty Augustus and worldwide taxation, how insignificant Joseph and Mary must have appeared! Yet the stream of God's purpose moved with them and Caesar Augustus was incidental. The true historian is he who can chart "His Story" in history. Compare Luke 3:2 and see John the Baptist against the window dressing of big names beginning with Tiberius Caesar. All that really matters is what God is doing. Man's busy little movements get the headlines, but they mean little except as they contribute to the outworking of God's great plan. The Bible is the textbook of God's history, disregarded in our educational system, but the only reliable explanation of the meaning of all other histories.

JANUARY 18

THE SUPERSCRIPTION

Jesus of Nazareth, the King of the Jews. . . . And it was written in Hebrew, and Greek, and Latin.   John 19:19, 20.

THE WORLD STAGE was set for the coming of the Saviour. There was the Roman world of government, the Greek world of culture, and the Hebrew world of religion. The Roman world had law and order, peace for a while, roads and commerce and means of communication. The Greek world had a flexible language for the propogation of the Gospel. The Hebrew world had one God and looked for the Messiah. The superscription on the cross bore witness that this was no accident of history, but the stage setting for Him who alone gives meaning to history.

JANUARY 19

THE SECRET OF DESTINY

Who is worthy to open the book . . . ?   Revelation 5:2.

ONLY JESUS CHRIST can open the seals and unroll the meaning of history. Mr. Durant and Mr. Toynbee do not have the key. Without Jesus Christ, secular history is only a tale told by a fool, full of sound and fury and signifying absolutely nothing. It is well to know the facts of history and God makes them fit into His design. Today truth may seem forever on the scaffold and wrong forever on the throne, but behind the dim unknown standeth God within the shadow keeping watch above His own. And, to those who are His own, all things work together for good, for they are the called according to His purpose— His purpose for the individual and for creation.

JANUARY 20

WEEP NOT FOR ME

Weep not for me. . . .   Luke 23:28.

THERE ARE THOSE today who make a show of sympathy for the suffering Saviour, especially on Good Friday. He bids us still, "Weep not for me." He did not climb Calvary's hill as the helpless victim of a mob. He could have called down twelve legions of angels. He went up the slopes of Golgotha on purpose to give His life as a ransom for many. We had better weep for ourselves and our children. Things are in a bad way for us and them. Judgment looms ahead and our Lord is saying, "If they do these things in a green tree, what shall they do in the dry?" Then, the fall of Jerusalem lay ahead, today the end of the age.

JANUARY 21

WHY WEEPEST THOU?

Why weepest thou? John 20:15.

MARY WEPT BECAUSE she could not find the body of her Lord. She was seeking the living among the dead. So do we today. But we do not worship at the tomb of a dead Saviour. The Emmaus disciples trudged along a lonely road in sadness. It was the third day since His Crucifixion and, since it was, they should have been singing instead of sighing for He had promised to rise on that very day!

When Mary did see the Lord, she thought He was the gardener. We shall make all kinds of mistakes until we believe in a risen Saviour. Mary was synonymous with misery until she recognized Him as Master. Then He gave her a message and a mission. Let us dry our tears and tell it everywhere, "He lives!"

JANUARY 22

AND I WEPT MUCH

And I wept much. . . . Revelation 5:4.

JOHN WEPT BECAUSE no man was found worthy to open the scroll and loose its seals. But one of the elders said, "Weep not." The Lion of the tribe of Juda would solve the problem! When John looked, he saw not a Lion but a Lamb. It is not as a conquering Lion but as a suffering Lamb that our Lord prevailed. One day He will return as the Lion in judgment to avenge His own elect. This is God's history within history, the redemption of man and the whole creation. Bewildered men might well weep today that no man can unravel the future, but there is an answer: "Worthy is the Lamb!"

JANUARY 23

JOY COMETH IN THE MORNING

Jesus wept.　　John 11:35.

SOME SAY HE wept because raising Lazarus meant bringing him back into a world of sorrow and suffering. He certainly was identifying with our grief. We are to weep with them that weep, yet not sorrow as those who have no hope. Our Lord asked, "Why?" that we might never ask it. "Weeping may endure for a night, but joy cometh in the morning" (Psalms 30:5). "There shall be no more . . . crying" (Revelation 21:4). God shall wipe all tears from our eyes. I am glad He gives it His personal attention!

JANUARY 24

ONLY WEEP PURPOSEFULLY

A time to weep. . . .　　Ecclesiastes 3:4.

WE DO WELL to weep for ourselves and our children, for the sad state of the Church, and for a lost world. It is well to weep when dear ones depart. God does not despise human grief. It is a safety valve in sorrow. The Psalmist prayed that his tears might be put in God's bottle. Not a tear worthily shed is ever lost though we seem to weep in vain. But shed no tears that serve no purpose. Weep not seeking the living among the dead. Weep not because men cannot read the meaning of history and the secret of destiny. And press on toward the day when God shall dry our tears forever!

JANUARY 25

BEHIND THE MASK

Why feignest thou thyself to be another? 1 Kings 14:6.

AMERICA IS LAUGHING itself to death in a vain attempt to drown its sorrows and forget its fears. Behind a thin veneer of hilarity, there are more broken homes, hearts, minds, and lives than ever in our history. After preaching for sixty years, I am not deceived by the masks we wear in church on Sunday morning. Many a smile is only a front to hide the marks of a sleepless night and many a poker face conceals a pressure-cooker mind about to explode. One night in my meetings, a man was awarded a prize for bringing the most people to church only to go home and hang himself. This wild and weary world is a weeping world, no matter how cleverly it hides its grief.

JANUARY 26

HE HATH BORNE OUR GRIEFS

Acquainted with grief. . . . Isaiah 53:3.

NEVER FORGET THAT Christianity began with a Man of sorrows acquainted with grief. Joel called on God's ministers to weep between the porch and the altar. Paul warned everyone day and night with tears. The joy of the Lord is not to be confused with the religious levity that has no root or depth. Churches have become second-class theaters as though the Gospel were a form of entertainment. The joy of the Lord is not a "happenness" that depends on what happens. It smiles through tears and rejoices in spite of what happens.

JANUARY 27

WEEPING HEREAFTER

Weeping and gnashing of teeth.   Matthew 25:30.

THE MOST GRUESOME details about the future state of the wicked come from the lips of our Lord Himself. Call it imagery, symbolism, what you will, it is a fearful picture and we dare not tone it down or call it an accommodation to the prevailing ideas of the time. Dives in hell was a personality in torment and anguish with memory intact. The word *lost* has almost disappeared from our vocabulary and any mention of eternal punishment is smiled away as a leftover from a dark theological past. There will be tears throughout eternity in remorse and regret for the lost opportunity to have been in heaven instead of hell.

JANUARY 28

THE UNEQUAL YOKE

Be ye not unequally yoked together with unbelievers. . . .
2 Corinthians 6:14.

THE CHRISTIAN AND the Church must not accept the help of the world in the work of God. This world has neither part nor lot in the matter. When we accept subsidy, we surrender sovereignty. The man who pays the fiddler calls the tune. The assistance of the world has its price. There are strings to it and out of these strings a noose is formed. It is the strategy of the devil to join churches these days, not fight them, and gradually to control them. It is the policy of false teachers. Even the state by subsidizing religious education achieves the same ends.

JANUARY 29

F-A-I-T-H

According to your faith be it unto you.   Matthew 9:29.

I LIKE TO make an acrostic of that little word *F-A-I-T-H*. FOR ALL I TAKE HIM. FOR ALL I TRUST HIM. FOR ALL I THANK HIM. FOR ALL He Is I TAKE HIM. FOR ALL My Need I TRUST HIM. FOR ALL His Gifts I THANK HIM.

I do not just take Him *as* this or that. I take Him! He is Alpha and Omega and all the letters between. "As many as received him . . ." (John 1:12)—period!

JANUARY 30

THE CHIRST OF THE LONELY ROAD

He was alone. . . .   Luke 9:18.

E. STANLEY JONES wrote *The Christ of the Indian Road.* It had a wide circulation and was followed by various books about the Christ of other roads. My Lord was also the Christ of the Lonely Road, often in solitude, persecuted, misunderstood, crying at last on a cross, "My God, my God, why hast thou forsaken me?"

We who follow in His steps find that the way is not crowded. "Few there be that find it" (Matthew 7:14). But we are not alone though often lonely. "Lo, I am with you . . ." (Matthew 28:20).

And His road is the *only road.* "No man cometh unto the Father, but by me" (John 14:6).

JANUARY 31

COMMUNICATION AND COMMUNION

Compassed about with so great a cloud of witnesses. . . .
Hebrews 12:1.

WE CANNOT COMMUNICATE with the dead, but the communion of saints includes all past, present, and future believers—the family of the children of God. The cloud of witnesses holds us in full survey and we can sometimes feel the Presence we cannot touch. We are all in Him though we are on this side and they on the other. How much they see and know of what goes on here we may not know, but they see from the other world—as God sees—so what might disturb them if they were here, gives them no pain.

FEBRUARY 1

THE CROSS, VERTICAL AND HORIZONTAL

Love the Lord thy God. . . . [and] thy neighbour as thyself.
Matthew 22:37, 39.

THE CROSS IS both vertical and horizontal. The vertical God-and-man relationship is taken care of. Man is reconciled to God by the propitiatory death of God's Son and the Judgment Seat is now a Mercy Seat. We are made right with God. But often Christians are not in fellowship with the Father; there is rebellion against the will of God. Is there something between your soul and the Saviour? Then there may be something between you and somebody else and man must be reconciled to man. Are you right vertically and horizontally, loving God and your neighbor?

FEBRUARY 2

GOD PROVIDED SOME BETTER THING FOR US

And others. . . .   Hebrews 11:25.

THE FORMIDABLE ARRAY of God's heroes in this Westminster Abbey of the Bible is followed by another category of those for whom things went the other way. For them there were no miracles, no marvelous answers to prayer, no deliverance—only torture and mockings and scourgings and bonds and imprisonments. Slain by the sword, sawn asunder, stoned, tempted, wanderers in sheepskins and goatskins, destitute, afflicted, tormented—what wretched misery! And greater still than the misery is the mystery, why? Why do some achieve such outstanding feats of faith while for others everything seems to go wrong? We do not know. But we do know that all of it works together for good to God's people.

FEBRUARY 3

THE MIRACLE OF IT

And we know that all things work together for good to them that love God, to them who are the called according to his purpose.
Romans 8:28.

THE MISERY OF these "others" in Hebrews 11:35–38 appals us. The *mystery* of it bewilders us. But we rejoice in the *miracle* of it, that God can take these awful things that befall these saints and weave a tapestry glorious on the heavenly side although full of loose ends and ragged edges on our side. Only God could do it but He does. When we no longer see through a glass as in a riddle, *misery and mystery will give way to the finished miracle.* Whether we are listed in the chronicles of the celebrities or the annals of the anonymous "others" not even named, our times are in His hand.

FEBRUARY 4

MINUS AND PLUS

In the year that King Uzziah died I saw also the Lord. . . .
Isaiah 6:1.

THE DEATH OF King Uzziah was a national calamity. Everybody was overwhelmed. Isaiah was stunned, but with the minus there was a plus: he saw also the Lord. Everybody else saw the disaster. Isaiah saw it, too, but he saw more. There are minuses aplenty today. We see not yet all things put under Him, but there is a plus, we see Jesus.

Blessed is the man for whom the minuses bring also a plus, a vision of the Lord.

FEBRUARY 5

RUBBISH

There is much rubbish. . . .   Nehemiah 4:10.

ON ANY CONSTRUCTION site there is always much rubbish while the building is going up. Broken pieces, odds and ends, leftovers clutter the scene. But when the work is done and the building is up, all the trash is carted away. The new edifice stands clean and complete. In this present age, God's building plans are not finished and there is much rubbish, much that is not necessary to the ultimate completion of His purpose. Like the builders of Nehemiah's time, we grow weary and discouraged and we complain that we are not able to build the wall. There are many broken fragments that do not fit the blueprints. But we must not begin to build and fail to finish, for One who has begun a good work will perform it until the day of Jesus Christ.

FEBRUARY 6

THE ORIGINAL PURPOSE OF GOD

And God saw every thing that he had made, and, behold, it was very good. Genesis 1:31.

GOD'S ORIGINAL PURPOSE was to create an Edenic Paradise with man in charge, living in peace and plenty with nature in harmony, without sin and suffering, disease and death. He did just that and the Bible begins with that idyllic, peaceable kingdom which men have dreamed about and longed for ever since. But Satan spoiled that first Creation. Sin entered and nature came under the bondage of corruption and now groans and longs, standing on tiptoe waiting for the restoration of Paradise.

FEBRUARY 7

THE PRESENT PURPOSE OF GOD

To take out . . . a people for his name. Acts 15:14.

GOD BEGAN AGAIN with a chosen people of His own, Israel, and then a purchased people, the Church. He is not saving civilization. He sent His Son to reconcile us to Himself and to be the Adam of a new race of as many as received Him. These He foreknows, predestinates, calls, justifies, and glorifies and His purpose is to conform them to the image of His Son. For them all things work together for good for they are "the called according to his purpose" (Romans 8:28).

FEBRUARY 8

GOD'S ULTIMATE PURPOSE

Behold, I make all things new.   Revelation 21:5.

GOD'S ULTIMATE PURPOSE at the end of the age is to establish His
Kingdom on earth, the new Paradise, to reign in Christ over a re-
deemed Creation, and beyond that to create a new heaven and earth.
This is that divine event toward which the whole Creation moves. The
glorious prospect of all God's children who are called according to
His present purpose to share eternity in that ultimate purpose!

FEBRUARY 9

THE EMPTY HEART

And they enter in and dwell there.   Matthew 12:43–45.

AN EMPTY HEART is an invitation to the devil. It may not be an evil
heart. An evil heart, deceitful and desperately wicked, is already
occupied by Satan. An empty heart may be swept out and gar-
nished; some bad habit may have been dropped, some new resolution made. One may even make some sort of Christian profession
and join a church, but unless Jesus Christ takes up His abode in the
vacated heart, seven demons return and the last state is worse than
the first.

FEBRUARY 10

BE RIGHT

Renew a right spirit within me.   Psalms 51:10.

THE NATURAL HEART is not right in the sight of God. It is deceitful
above all things and desperately wicked. We are right with God only
in the imputed, imparted, implanted righteousness of Christ. "There

is a way which seemeth right unto a man, but the end thereof are the ways of death" (Proverbs 14:12). We are rightly related to God by the death of Christ who met the demands of God's righteousness, took our sin upon Him, and died, the Just for the unjust, that God might be both just and justifier of all who believe. Dr. Torrey used to advertise his meetings with a big placard saying, GET RIGHT WITH GOD.

FEBRUARY 11

BE RICH

That ye . . . might be rich.   2 Corinthians 8:9.

NOT GET RICH—a man's life consists not in his possessions (Luke 12:15). But we can *be* rich in Christ Jesus who became poor that we through His poverty might be rich. He bids us buy of Him gold tried in the fire that we may be rich (Revelation 3:18). Laodicea said, "I am rich" and was poor. Smyrna was poor but rich in the eyes of the Lord (Revelation 2:9). No church should seek to get rich but rather to *be* rich, possessing its possessions, being what it is, laying up treasure in heaven—gold tried in the fire.

FEBRUARY 12

BE RADIANT

They looked unto him, and were lightened: and their faces were not ashamed.   Psalms 34:5.
We all, with open face beholding as in a glass the glory of the Lord, are changed into the same image from glory to glory, even as by the Spirit of the Lord.   2 Corinthians 3:18.

THE BECOMING FOLLOWS the beholding. The likeness follows the looking. It is a glow, not a shine painted on from without. Alas, for

27

so much of the Church the glory, the radiance, has departed. Many a sanctuary is only an Ichabod Memorial! When we are right and rich by God's standard, we shall be radiant.

FEBRUARY 13

BE READY

Be ye also ready. . . .   Matthew 24:44.

NOT ONLY READY for His coming or ready to die but ready for anything—ready to give an answer for the hope within us (1 Peter 3:15), ready to preach the Gospel (Romans 1:15). The Christian should live in a state of constant readiness to live or die, to spend or be spent. Ready to die and therefore ready to live. Ready to live and therefore ready to die. Paul had only two days on his calendar, "Today" and "That day." The Christian who is right and rich and radiant is ready, come what may!

FEBRUARY 14

MY GOD, WHY?

My God, my God, why hast thou forsaken me?
Matthew 27:46.

ONE OF THE words most often on the lips of children is *Why?* And from then on, we question the Almighty: "Why did this happen to me?" We behold the tragedy and the mystery, the iniquities and the inequities of life. We cannot add it up. It does not make sense. Even our Lord said once, "Now is my soul troubled; and what shall I say?" (John 12:27). But it was on the cross that He cried, "My God, WHY . . . ?" He asked it that we might never ask it. If we could fathom all that is wrapped up in that moment when God's Son became our sin and a holy God turned His back, we would have the answer to all our *Whys.*

28

FEBRUARY 15

TO GO OR TO STAY

A desire to depart . . . nevertheless to abide. . . .
Philippians 1:23, 24.

WE WHO ARE homesick for heaven long to be with Christ "which is far better." But we may be needed here a while longer so there is the *nevertheless.* Ready to go, ready to stay—that is the Christian's attitude. God knows where we belong today. The desire to get away from it all is not always mere escapism. This world is our proving ground and is ideal for that purpose. It takes the grindstone to sharpen the axe. There is an understandable longing to fly away as a dove and be at rest, but only in God's time is it Christian.

FEBRUARY 16

OUR LIFE

I am . . . the life. . . . John 14:6. *Christ, who is our life. . . .*
Colossians 3:4.

IT REMAINS TO be seen what would happen if we who trust Christ as Saviour and Lord would also take Him as our life. We have a new life which is Christ Himself and there is no limit to what might be ours if we could simply trust Him for every need of body, mind, and spirit. This does not rule out the use of means but puts everything in His care. He is the life for the total man and when we say, "Christ liveth in me," and "To me to live is Christ," we are in a new dimension. There is only one Christian life, Christ Himself, but He lives it again in us according to His Word and will, our need and our faith.

FEBRUARY 17

IT MAY BE SOON

Shortly I must put off this my tabernacle. . . . 2 Peter 1:14.

I REMEMBER HEARING long ago an old song about dying: "It won't be long, It may be soon." Some of us draw near to another shore. It can't be long, it may be soon. With more dear ones there than here, that other land beckons. We grow more and more attached to that world, and this one loses its charm by the day. Along with unworldliness there should be otherworldliness for our citizenship is there, not here.

It won't be long, it may be soon!

FEBRUARY 18

SEEKING A CITY

He looked for a city which hath foundations, whose builder and maker is God. . . . They seek a country. . . . God . . . hath prepared for them a city. Hebrews 11:10, 14, 16.

ABRAHAM LOOKED FOR a city and all who follow in his train seek a country. They are self-confessed strangers, pilgrims on the earth. Their quest is not in vain for God has prepared for them a city. Abraham's tent knew no secure foundations, only pegs driven in the desert sand. The gates of God's city are open to those who do His commandments (Revelation 22:14).

We read that the voyagers with Paul deemed that they drew near to some country (Acts 27:27). We are nearing that City and that Country!

FEBRUARY 19

AVERAGE

Thou art lukewarm, and neither cold nor hot. . . .
Revelation 3:16.

AVERAGE HAS BEEN defined as the best of the worst and the worst of the best. Our Lord would have us cold rather than lukewarm. He would have us "zealous," boiling. But we need not boil so violently that we blow off the lid! The tendency is to swing from subnormal to abnormal. *Normal* does not mean average. Average run-of-the-mill Christianity is our main problem. We have confused lukewarmness with the norm. The vast majority of Sunday-morning parishioners take pride in being middle-of-the-roaders. The New Testament Christian lives above the average.

FEBRUARY 20

ABOUNDING

God is able to make all grace abound toward you; that ye, always having all sufficiency in all things, may abound to every good work. . . . 2 Corinthians 9:8.

GOD ABOUNDS AND we abound. There will always be enough of all we need to do all that God wants us to do as long as He wants us to do it.

Then why pray? We do not have some things because we do not ask for them. The true father provides for the needs of his children, but they ask for other things and receive extras because they ask. Our Father gives liberally and does not upbraid. He abounds that we may abound.

FEBRUARY 21

IDLE WORSHIP

In vain do they worship me. . . . Matthew 15:9.

IDOL WORSHIP IN Africa is no worse than idle worship in America.

> All is vain unless the Spirit
> Of the Holy One comes down.
> GEORGE ATKINS

God was disgusted with idle worship in Israel. Amos ridiculed it in Bethel. Our Lord was nauseated with the lukewarmness of Laodicea. Sunday-morning Christianity is the greatest hindrance to true revival. Experience has become mere performance, "a form of godliness, but denying the power thereof . . ." (2 Timothy 3:5).

FEBRUARY 22

TOP MAN ON THE TOTEM POLE

And there was also a strife among them, which of them should be accounted the greatest.   Luke 22:24.

AT NO TIME did Jesus seek fame or prestige or position. He kept His miracles secret, did not stage performances in Jerusalem, sought no earthly eminence. How this contrasts with the race in the ministry for the big church, the top seat in the synagogue! It is the American itch for place and power and it gets over into the Church. Political scrambling for influence, preeminence—this is as evident in religion as elsewhere. But should we not have ambition? Only to be in the place of God's choosing, great or small—that and that only is success in God's Book!

FEBRUARY 23

THEN THE LORD

When my father and my mother forsake me, then the Lord will take me up. Psalms 27:10.

MY FATHER AND mother went to heaven long ago. My dearest wife left this world some time ago. Almost all of my immediate family live on the other side. But God remains and I am not alone. Those I love have not left me forever. I am just lagging behind a little! Forsaken? Yes, for a moment. Then the Lord! "I will never leave thee, nor forsake thee."

FEBRUARY 24

WHICH ADAM IS IN CHARGE?

Put ye on the Lord Jesus Christ, and make not provision for the flesh, to fulfil the lusts thereof. Romans 13:14.

ARE YOU AWARE of two forces striving within: the old Adam doubting and fearing, the new man believing and rejoicing? In the Christian, both are present and we shift gears back and forth. It should not be so. We should walk habitually in the Spirit although there may be occasional lapses back into the flesh. Such lapses should be accidents on the trip, possible but not on the schedule! Make no provision for the flesh, leave no loopholes, nothing that makes sinning more likely. Live in the New Adam and the Old Adam will grow weaker. Which Adam is in charge?

FEBRUARY 25

ARMISTICE

Have no fellowship with the unfruitful works of darkness, but rather reprove them. Ephesians 5:11.

I HAVE JUST been reading a book written forty years ago by a prominent minister. It condemns, in the light of Scripture, liquor, dancing, the movies, card playing, and other evils in no uncertain terms. Today such preaching is condemned even by the clergy. Many of them participate in such evils or at least smile upon them in tolerance and permissiveness. Our churches live at an armistice in peaceful coexistence with the world, the flesh, and the devil.

FEBRUARY 26

LONELY

No man cared for my soul. Psalms 142:4.

ONE OF THE worst things about loneliness is that you can't run away from it. Wherever you go, there is your loneliness sticking closer than a brother. Today a generation without inner resources is driven crazy trying to find ways of avoiding its own company. Radio or television must be turned on, some resort to drugs or drink, every device under the sun is called upon to circumvent loneliness. What a commentary on ourselves that we find *us* unendurable! What a poor creature is myself if I can't stand *me!* A mind stored with good treasure and a heart at peace with God and man can be lived with by its possessor. Better still, Christ dwells within and who then can possibly be lonely!

FEBRUARY 27

NEARER HOME

The night is far spent, the day is at hand. . . . Romans 13:12.

SOMEHOW, AS I strolled after supper today, it came to me with overwhelming force, "You're one day nearer home than ever before." One day nearer the dawning when the fogs will lift, mysteries clear, and all question marks straighten up into exclamation points! I shall see the King! I wonder what my dear ones will look like between death and the resurrection. I stand on tiptoe with the whole creation, waiting. I'm a whole day nearer home!

FEBRUARY 28

FEW

Strait is the gate, and narrow is the way, which leadeth unto life, and few there be that find it. Matthew 7:14.

IN THIS DAY when our faith has been diluted and cheapened, when almost everybody in the congregation belongs to a church (I could have led some to Christ if they hadn't joined a church!)—in such a time as this, when many think there is really not much to being a Christian, we need a good jolt. This verse ought to give it. Our Lord plainly says that compared to the multitude on the wide road to destruction only a few will travel the old S and N, the Straight and Narrow Way. That road has never been widened. Few there be that find it.

FEBRUARY 29

NOT MUCH ABOVE WET-SHOD.

When thou passest through the waters, I will be with thee; and through the rivers, they shall not overflow thee. . . .   Isaiah 43:2.

MR. FEARING IN *Pilgrim's Progress* was always afraid he would never make it to the Celestial City he had come so far to behold. When he reached the river of death, God had the waters so low that the timid pilgrim made it "not much above wet-shod."

So we sing, "When I tread the verge of Jordan, Bid my anxious fears subside." We should not be fearful or uneasy because God knows our frame and remembers that we are dust.

MARCH 1

PRECIOUS MEMORIES

Oh that I were as in months past. . . .   Job 29:2.

NOTHING IS MORE precious after a loved one has gone than the recollection of countless memories that troop into our lonely hearts from days forever past. Sweet little happenings, things we shared that mean nothing to anybody else, how they linger! Utterly trivial and insignificant except to us, they help us to relive hours we never valued then as we do now in retrospect. Little run-of-the-mill things we said and did now loom large for little keys unlock big doors.

William Jennings Bryan said, "Christ has made of death a narrow starlit strip between the companionships of yesterday and the reunions of tomorrow." Like butterflies, precious memories dance along that trail!

MARCH 2

FLYING BY INSTRUMENT

The things which shall be hereafter. . . . Revelation 1:19.

WHEN ALL IS said and done, there is absolutely only one authority on the life to come. Surmisings of pagans and speculations of philosophers mean nothing. It is the Bible or else. It may have its difficult passages, may leave questions unanswered, but all we know about the next world is told between the covers of this old Book.

Sometimes the airplane pilot can see nothing and must fly by instrument. The Christian must often do the same and that instrument is the Word of God. It guarantees a safe landing!

MARCH 3

IN OUR DAY

And as it was in the days of Noe. . . . in the days of Lot. . . . thus shall it be. . . . Luke 17:26,28,30.

WHAT WERE THEY doing then? Our Lord does not say that they were gambling, carousing. They were eating and drinking, marrying and giving in marriage, buying and selling, planting and building. These are normal and legitimate pursuits if carried on properly, but, if they engage all our time and interest, then it becomes worldliness. Listen to most people talk and these things are the subjects of their conversation. If these things are their life then they are just as unready for our Lord's return as are the immoral, indecent, and criminal brackets of society. The people of Noah's and Lot's day *knew not*. So shall it be and so it is today.

MARCH 4

UNLIKELY PLACES

Which is desert.   Acts 8:26.

STRANGE ORDERS WERE given to Philip to leave a great awakening in Samaria and head for a desert! God's itinerary for us lists what sometimes seems to be the most unlikely and unpromising places. We do not always do our best work where circumstances are most propitious. In the springtime, I have found fewest birds in elegant parks and gardens. They are more likely to show up in a swamp. I have planned mornings of meditation in favored spots and nothing came of it. The angels come down, as with Jacob at Bethel when his pillow was a stone that became a pillar! A desert assignment may find a prospect for the Gospel well worth the trip!

MARCH 5

HITHERTO AND HENCEFORTH

Hitherto hath the Lord helped us.   1 Samuel 7:12. *The Lord is round about his people from henceforth even for ever.*
Psalms 125:2.

RETROSPECT REVEALS THAT God has never failed us. Up to now He has been our Helper. "Can I doubt His tender mercy who through life has been my guide?" Elisha saw the angels camping round about to deliver them that fear Him. If we make our requests known with thanksgiving, the peace of God that passes all understanding will garrison our hearts and minds!

In old age, a lonely soul might fear the days ahead, but instead of panic there can be peace. Through many dangers, toils, and snares, we have already come. The grace for "thus far" will lead us home. There can be a life of rest for the rest of life.

MARCH 6

GIANTS AND GRASSHOPPERS

And there we saw the giants . . . and we were in our own sight as grasshoppers, and so we were in their sight. Numbers 13:33.

WHEN GOD DESCRIBED the Promised Land as flowing with milk and honey, He also said it was the place of the Canaanites, Hittites, Amorites, Perizzites, Hivites, and Jebusites. When the spies returned from viewing the land, they confirmed the description. The Christian life is a land of promise, but it is peopled with adversaries. Canaan is not heaven. All is not milk and honey. There are giants of Anak, but they should not make us feel we are grasshoppers. If we think we are grasshoppers, they will agree with our thinking!

MARCH 7

REST

I will give you rest. Matthew 11:28.

I HEARD RECENTLY about a dear brother who prayed, "Lord, give us more rest than time will allow." With most of us, there is not time enough to rest as much as we should. The modern pace takes its toll. Of course we could eliminate many nonessentials and save precious hours. When we have done that and still there is not time enough, God gives us extra strength. If we cannot go away for a vacation, we can take an "inside vacation" and find grace to help in time of need. God gives more rest than time will allow!

MARCH 8

SEND FOR DANIEL!

Now let Daniel be called. . . . Daniel 5:12.

DANIEL WAS NOT present as a guest at the feast of Belshazzar. He did not belong to the club and had no complimentary ticket to the orgy. He did not even drink ginger ale among the alcoholics! But he ended up the most honored of all because he was where he belonged until he was sent for. If more prophets stayed where they belong, they would be summoned when God writes on the wall. It is fashionable nowadays for the clergy to attend the suppers of Sodom and the grog-fests of Babylon, but they cannot decipher the heavenly hieroglyphics in the hour of doom.

MARCH 9

COULD OR CAN?

For the eyes of the Lord run to and fro throughout the whole earth, to shew himself strong in the behalf of them whose heart is perfect toward him. 2 Chronicles 16:9.

THERE IS NO use praying "Lord, use me." He *is* using us all He *can* but not all He *could.* All He can under the circumstances, but not all He could if we were more usable. God is shorthanded and looking for helpers. The harvest is plenteous and the laborers are few. He wants to show *Himself* strong in our behalf, not *us* strong in His behalf. He is on the lookout and He will use us to the extent that we are usable. Move over from what He *can* do now to what He *could* do!

MARCH 10

RALLYING THE REMNANT

Yet I have left me seven thousand in Israel, all the knees which have not bowed unto Baal, and every mouth which hath not kissed him. 1 Kings 19:18.

IT IS EASY to get under the juniper and fancy, "I am the sole surviving saint." But God has His faithful remnant and our biggest business is to rally it. There are more than seven thousand who do not bow to Baal. God keeps the books and knows them that are His. Here is the real witness today. We cannot organize it, but we can challenge and revive it and out of this kindling wood start a fire.

MARCH 11

JESUS AND HIS PROSPECTS

If any man will come after me. . . .   Matthew 16:24.

JESUS DID NOT pressure people into following Him. He began with an *If* and simply stated the terms. He did not encourage superficial enthusiasm. To three prospective disciples (Luke 9:57–62), He spoke in terms that seem harsh. He dealt firmly and almost severely with the Uncounted Cost, the Unburied Corpse, and the Unforsaken Circle. He spoke of those who hear the Word and receive it with joy but have no root or depth. He did not accept the Rich Young Ruler instantly as we would have done. There were sober *Ifs* and stern requirements.

MARCH 12

BREAKTHROUGH

Oh that thou wouldst rend the heavens, that thou wouldest come down. . . . Isaiah 64:1.

THE SCOFFERS OF this world say, "All things continue as they were from the beginning of the creation" (2 Peter 3:4). Things run a course fixed by natural law. Everything is simply cause and effect. God never breaks through. But some of us know that He has broken through in His Word, in His Son, at Pentecost, in regeneration, in revival, in answered prayer—not *contra*naturally but *super*naturally. He is not locked up in His own universe, the prisoner of His own laws. He does not break but transcends them when it suits His purpose. He does break through!

MARCH 13

THE SECRET OF CONFIDENCE

Beloved, if our heart condemn us not, then have we confidence toward God. 1 John 3:21.

THE PRECEDING VERSE in this passage says that God knows everything. He knows the heart and it is the heart that matters. God knows the inner intent, the real direction of our lives, what in our innermost selves we want to be and do. We may stumble and fall, make mistaken decisions, but He knows the truth about us. We often misjudge others because we do not know their hearts.

> What's done we partly may compute
> But know not what's resisted.

So we come with confidence and are promised answers to our prayers for God knows when we really seek to know and do His will.

MARCH 14

GOD'S DELIGHT

He delighteth in mercy.   Micah 7:18.

THE NOTION THAT God is a harsh judge, breathing vengeance and judgment on broken and wayward men, is utterly foreign to His nature. True, He hates sin and His wrath blazes on stubborn, willful wickedness. But when we are frustrated and in a dilemma, He does not turn from us fed up and furious. He delighteth in mercy and "as the heaven is high above the earth, so great is his mercy toward them that fear him" (Psalms 103:11). This does not encourage careless living as though God were an indulgent, grandfatherly being winking at our wickedness but neither does it drive the erring child to despair.

MARCH 15

LET GOD MANAGE YOUR AFFAIRS

He shall choose our inheritance for us. . . .   Psalms 47:4.

WE ARE TRYING continually to make ourselves secure, buying stocks and bonds, making investments, insuring life and property. The true Christian lets God make his choices—lays up his treasure in heaven. We try to gain support from people, leaning on the arm of flesh. But even best friends fail us, loved ones die, money runs out, investments fail. Better let God manage your affairs and select your investments. Trust Him about health, husband or wife, lifework, finances, where to spend time and strength. His stocks never fail, His bank never breaks.

MARCH 16

GOD NEVER COMES NEXT

Suffer me first. . . . Luke 9:59. *Seek ye first. . . .*
Matthew 6:33.

THE PROSPECTIVE DISCIPLE thought he must first take care of his father. "After that," he was saying in effect, "You will be next." But our Lord never comes *next.* He does not play second fiddle. God does not take second place. "Thou shalt have no other gods before me." Jesus is not only first but also last, Alpha and Omega. Attending early church services to celebrate the Lord's Day only to desecrate the rest of that day is not putting God first, it is only a way of getting rid of Him! God is a jealous God. Seek Him first and all else we need will be added.

MARCH 17

IS JESUS ALL YOU WANT?

Ye are complete in him. . . . Colossians 2:10.

WE DO NOT usually learn that Christ is all we need until we reach that place where He is all we have! Then He is all we want! As long as we have props to lean upon, we do not feel a desperate need of Him. Utter destitution brings complete dependence. The Rich Young Ruler had his money and so he never found in Christ his every need.

When Jesus is all you have, He will be all you need and want. Then we are poor in spirit and heirs of the Kingdom. Then we have nothing and possess all things. Suffering the loss of all things, we find the meaning of: All things are yours and ye are Christ's and Christ is God's.

MARCH 18

TWELVE BARRELS OF WATER

And the water ran round about the altar. . . .   1 Kings 18:35.

ELIJAH DOUSED THE altar with water so that if any fire kindled upon it, that fire must come from heaven. He did not warm up the altar with a little fire so that God would not have a hard time adding the flame from above!

A drenched altar is a sorry sight, but it is only the drenched altar that God sets on fire. When we get to the place where it can't be done unless God does it, God will do it! We must build the altar and prepare the sacrifice but we cannot kindle the flame. "All is vain unless the Spirit of the Holy One comes down."

MARCH 19

COME WHAT MAY

Not knowing the things that shall befall me. . . .   Acts 20:22.

SOMETHING GOOD MAY happen to you today. On the other hand, it may be something bad. "Fore-fancy your deathbed" is good advice, but you cannot make a pattern of the dying experiences of the saints. Moody died with a glimpse of heaven, but others just as mature went out under a cloud and some in dismal and tragic circumstances. The brain can be diseased just like the liver and the last moments of life may best be forgotten. Come what may, we will trust and not be afraid.

MARCH 20

ACCEPTANCE

The Lord gave, and the Lord hath taken away; blessed be the name of the Lord. Job 1:21.

WE ARE INDEED to submit ourselves to God (James 4:7), but such submission does not mean craven cringing as under a tyrant. God is not a taskmaster but our Father. When trials come, we may submit because we have to and there is nothing else we can do. A better word here is *acceptance*. We accept God's dealings as Job did though we may not understand. It is not mere resignation to what cannot be helped but taking what comes, convinced that it is part of the "all things" that work together for our good.

MARCH 21

ALL WE NEED TO KNOW

He [*the Spirit of truth*] *will guide you into all truth. . . .*
John 16:13.

GOD DOES NOT tell us all we want to know about anything, but He will tell us all we need to know. There is so much here and hereafter that is hidden in mystery. There are unanswered *whys* and strange developments that make no sense. But we can know enough to carry us through the fog until we no longer see through a glass as in a riddle. We know, for instance, that He will keep what we have deposited with Him. We know that all things are working together for good to us in whom He is working out His purpose. That is enough to get through the mists of today to the morning of tomorrow.

46

MARCH 22

NOTHING JUST HAPPENS

My times are in thy hand. . . .   Psalms 31:15.

RECENTLY I HEARD a fine young preacher say, "God may *make* it happen, He may *let* it happen, but nothing just happens outside His sovereign will." It may be His directive will, it may be His permissive will, but it is never outside the range of His will. He may allow what He did not plan or originate, but, for the Christian, He can make whatever happens work in the overall pattern to conform us to the image of His Son. The devil can go no farther than God permits. Our times are in His hand and we are graven upon the palms of His hands. He has every situation well in hand!

MARCH 23

GOD WITH US

God with us.   Isaiah 7:14; Matthew 1:23.

ONE OF THE names of our Lord is Emmanuel, God With Us. We must get away from the notion that God is up there somewhere sending down a program for us to carry out. He is down here working for, in, and among His people. Our Lord did not die to placate an angry Deity. God was in Christ reconciling the world unto Himself. The Christian life is not something we try to live by God's help. Christ lives His life in all who can truly say, "To me to live is Christ." We do not do God's will by sheer determination and hard work. He works in us to will and to do of His good pleasure. It is all God's work with our consent and cooperation.

MARCH 24

IN BUSINESS WITH GOD

Labourers together with God. . . .   1 Corinthians 3:9.

I AM PROUD of the business I'm in and the Company I work for. The President is God's Son and His office door is always open so that a country preacher like myself can walk in, day or night, and talk to the Boss. I have stock in the Company and I've been cashing dividends for over sixty years. I've made my investment where banks don't break, that is mothproof, rustproof, where thieves do not break through and steal. I'm not just a member of the Firm; my Father is the Head of it and I'm a member of the Family! My bank can't fall, my business can't fail, because I'm a laborer with God!

MARCH 25

I WON'T BE HERE LONG

For what is your life? It is even a vapour, that appeareth for a little time, and then vanisheth away.   James 4:14.

EVEN THE HOUR of keenest pain or months of sad bereavement will one day seem but a fleeting moment. Time is relative. A few minutes in a medical examination may seem an hour while a young suitor's evening with his best girl friend may seem but a few minutes. "For our light affliction, which is but for a moment, worketh for us a far more exceeding and eternal weight of glory . . ." (2 Corinthians 4:17). Our threescore and ten years are short "for it is soon cut off, and we fly away" (Psalms 90:10). We won't be here long and we shall grieve that we misused our days and even the best shall regret that they did not spend them better.

MARCH 26

GROWING BY LEAPS AND BOUNDS

Grow up into him. . . .   Ephesians 4:15.

WE DO NOT grow in grace and the knowledge of Christ by leaps and bounds but some try. They bounce from one mountain peak of Christian experience to another. Every year or so they make a new start, turn a new leaf, have a new thrill. Children do not grow by suddenly gaining a few inches or adding a few pounds now and then. They grow gradually, daily, by food, rest, and exercise. Christian growth comes the same way by feeding on the Word, resting in the Lord, and exercising unto godliness. It has been said that nothing is more detrimental to Christian experience than too many Christian "experiences."

MARCH 27

CLEANSING THE TEMPLE

That he might sanctify and cleanse it. . . .   Ephesians 5:26.

AFTER JESUS CLEANSED the Temple, the lame and blind came and were healed. The children cried, "Hosanna." But the *celebration* followed the *cleansing.* The lame do not walk nor the blind see until the temple has been cleansed. We seek the blessings of revival without paying the cost of revival in repentance and confession of sin. Only after the joy of salvation has been restored and we have been purified are we ready to teach transgressors God's ways and see sinners converted.

MARCH 28

THE TIDE IS SURE TO WIN

*The earth shall be full of the knowledge of the Lord, as the waters
cover the sea.   Isaiah 11:9.*

I WALKED THE ocean beach today and watched the advance and
retreat of the waves, surging forward, then receding, but steadily
gaining ground. I remembered the poem with its lines:

> The wave may be defeated
> But the tide is sure to win.

If we are part of the purpose of God in the Gospel, we may advance
and recede, our wave may be defeated, but we are part of a movement
that must prevail. Better fail in a cause that will one day succeed than
succeed in a cause that will one day fail!

MARCH 29

AS GOOD AS DONE

*By faith Abraham, when he was tried, offered up Isaac. . . .
Hebrews 11:17.*

ABRAHAM DID NOT actually slay Isaac upon the altar, but God knew
his heart and took the will for the deed. It was as good as done. God
sometimes asks of us a sacrifice which He may not let us actually make
even as the Lord stayed Abraham's hand. The angel said, "Now I
know that thou fearest God, seeing thou hast not withheld thy son,
thine only son from me" (Genesis 22:12). What God looks for is the
intent of the heart and, when in our hearts we have already made the
sacrifice required, God may sometimes not ask us to actually finish
what we meant to do. Abraham put God first, not Isaac, and we read,

"In Isaac shall thy seed be called" (Genesis 21:12). Our testimony is perpetuated by the Isaac we offer at God's command, whether consummated actually or intentionally.

MARCH 30

ACCEPTING JESUS

The sacrifices of God are a broken spirit. . . .   Psalms 51:17.

INVITATIONS TO PROUD and haughty sinners often sound as though we were begging them to condescend to "accept" Christ as though doing Him a favor. The big question is, "Will He accept us?" Indeed He will ("Him that cometh to me I will in no wise cast out." John 6:37), but He is not standing, hat in hand, as though He were a bargain on an auction block. The New Testament word is not *accept,* but rather *believe, trust, receive, commit, follow,* and it requires a broken and contrite heart coming to the cross poor and weak and blind.

MARCH 31

IF—

If thou canst do any thing. . . . If thou canst believe. . . .
Mark 9:22,23.

MARTHA AND MARY said, "If thou hadst been here, my brother had not died" (John 11:21). Jesus said, "If thou wouldest believe, thou shouldest see the glory of God" (John 11:40). The father of the demonized boy had the wrong *if.* There are no *ifs* about what God can do. The *ifs* are on our side. That harassed father finally got around to the solution: "Lord, I believe, help thou mine unbelief" (Mark 9:24). He confessed unbelief but took sides with his faith. We are so inclined to say, "I doubt, help Thou my faith." We need to stop being *iffy* and be not faithless but believing.

APRIL 1

NIGHT WATCHMAN

Behold, he that keepeth Israel shall neither slumber nor sleep.
Psalms 121:4.

DARKNESS DOES NOT remove the beauty we see by day, it merely hides the mountains, the landscape, the flowers until morning. How good to know that God is awake by night as well as by day! Our loved ones whose lives are hidden with Christ in God are not destroyed by death, they are not lost. Death can hide but not divide, in Him we are united still. Because God is the Night Watchman of the Universe we can rest in the darkness while we await the dawn. There is the pillar of fire by night as well as the pillar of cloud by day.

APRIL 2

WALK BY FAITH

If we hope for that we see not, then do we with patience wait for it. Romans 8:25.

THAT IS THE reason a bird can sing—
On his darkest day he believes in spring.

The chickadee, the kinglet, the nuthatch, all the winter birds, keep up their chirping because they know by instinct that if winter comes, spring cannot be far behind. So the Christian sees the coming roses beyond the present snow. The sun is still there on a cloudy day, the mist hides but does not remove the mountain peaks. We walk by faith, not by sight.

APRIL 3

SATAN AMONG THE SONS OF GOD

*Now there was a day when the sons of God came to present
themselves before the Lord, and Satan came also among them.*
Job 1:6.

HERE IN DRAMATIC form we see the counterplay of two forces, Satan
appearing in the courts of heaven, God working for man's good and
the devil maneuvering for his downfall. The Book of Job reveals the
Prince of Darkness plotting a good man's destruction, but God bringing His servant's sad story to a happy ending, twice as blessed as his
beginning. Truth suffers on the scaffold, but "behind the dim unknown, standeth God within the shadow keeping watch above his
own."

APRIL 4

THE SIFTING OF THE SAINTS

*Simon, Simon, behold, Satan hath desired to have you, that he
may sift you as wheat: But I have prayed for thee, that thy faith
fail not: and when thou art converted, strengthen thy brethren.*
Luke 22:31,32.

HERE AGAIN ARE the countermovements of Satan and God. Satan
puts the saints in his sifter to winnow out the good and leave the bad.
Christ prays for His people that their testing may winnow out the
chaff and leave the wheat. The dross He would consume and the gold
refine. And all in order that the saint may be a strengthener of his
brethren. If you have not been through the devil's sifter, you are
probably not worth sifting!

APRIL 5

BUFFETINGS AND BLESSINGS

There was given to me a thorn in the flesh, the messenger of Satan to buffet me. . . . My strength is made perfect in weakness. 2 Corinthians 12:7,9.

ONCE AGAIN THE double action of evil versus good. Paul's thorn was not attributed to God but to its true source, the devil. We often try to pass the buck and ascribe to heaven what emanates from hell. We should glory in our infirmities but not glorify them. God may permit what He does not originate that all things, even evil things, may work together for our good.

APRIL 6

MIRACLES

In Isaac shall thy seed be called. Genesis 21:12. *Behold, a virgin shall conceive, and bear a son. . . .* Isaiah 7:14. *Born, not of blood, nor of the will of the flesh, nor of the will of man, but of God.* John 1:13.

EVERY JEW IS a miracle, descended from Isaac, who was born to Abraham and Sarah long past the age of parenthood. Jesus was a miracle baby born of a virgin. The true Church is made of people born again through faith in Christ. The Bible is a miracle book written by divine inspiration. No Christian has any business asking like Gideon, "Where be all the miracles?" We are part of the miracle business, the supernatural work of God.

APRIL 7

NO SMELL OF FIRE

Nor the smell of fire had passed on them.   Daniel 3:27.

WHEN THE THREE Hebrews came out of the fiery furnace, they had lost only the cords that had bound them. When we come through God's testing properly, all we lose are the shackles that tied us up earlier—we have been set free! And the smell of the smoke does not linger; there is no odor from the suffering. Instead, we have been purified and the perfume of a new holiness is soon detected. There is no lamenting over our losses or boasting of our survival—only the sweetness of a chastened spirit, the glow of gold refined after dross has been removed. Have you emerged from the furnace with no scorch, no shackles, no smell of the smoke?

APRIL 8

WE OUGHT TO MAKE A DIFFERENCE

Ye are the salt of the earth. . . . Ye are the light of the world.
Matthew 5:13,14.

AFTER READING IMPRESSIVE church statistics, who can help asking, "With this much salt, why is the country so corrupt? With this much light, why is America in such darkness?" We ought to make a difference. It does no good to say that we are in the last days; the world will not be converted and only a remnant will be saved. All that is true, but it can be made an excuse for the poor showing we are making in our day and time. Smaller statistics have moved society in the past. The Social Gospel will not do it but the Gospel has influenced and changed society as in the days of Wesley. The trouble is that the salt has lost its savor and the light is under the bushel and the bed.

APRIL 9

THE TWO APPEARINGS.

*It doth not yet appear what we shall be: but we know that,
when he shall appear, we shall be like him; for we shall see
him as he is.* 1 John 3:2.

EVERY TIME I look into a mirror I am reminded that it doth not yet
appear what I shall be! But when He appears, we shall put on our
Easter clothes! Some of us have laid away dear ones whose features
were so distorted and disfigured as to be hardly recognizable, but so
was our Lord when they laid Him away. His visage was so marred
that He did not look like a man. But He was marred that one day so
that all who are in Him shall rise unmarred. It does not appear so
now, but it will when He appears!

APRIL 10

EASTER OUTFIT

*Who shall change our vile body, that it may be fashioned like
unto his glorious body. . . .* Philippians 3:21.

THE BODY OF a Christian loved one is dear and—when laid away
unusable—is regarded with affection like a suit once thought becoming. This should not be with regret for that dear one now awaits an
Easter outfit! The resurrection brings a new wardrobe, a new suit for
the spirit, fashioned like the glorious body of our Lord, immune to
sickness, death, decay. It would be wonderful if Easter crowds throng-
ing the stores for new garments of the season could get as excited
about making sure of new garments on that Great Getting-Up Morning!

APRIL 11

ANTIQUES AND NOVELTIES

For all the Athenians and strangers ... spent their time in nothing else, but either to tell, or to hear some new thing. Acts 17:21.

THE CHURCH HAS gone Athenian, despising the antiques of the faith for modern novelties. We are in the biggest gadget and gimmick business in all our history. What we need is not something new but something so old that it would be new if anybody tried it! A return to the principles, program, and power of the old faith would be the greatest of innovations! Church services would not resemble the average meetings today. Nothing would be newer than the old faith if we gave it a chance.

APRIL 12

A WIND FROM ELSEWHERE

The wind bloweth where it listeth. ... John 3:8. *A sound from heaven as of a rushing mighty wind. ...* Acts 2:2.

WHEN A GREAT American city was enveloped by a smothering fog, a meteorologist said, "Only a sweep of wind from elsewhere can relieve this situation." Never has the world—and the Church—been so smogbound as today. Only a wind from elsewhere can clear up the situation. We can blow up quite a blast ourselves because we are so wired up with our own devices that, if there is no heavenly wind, we have machinery all set to blow hot air instead. Only the Holy Spirit, a wind from elsewhere, can disperse the fog.

NOT COMMUNITY BUT COMMUNION

Fellowcitizens with the saints. . . . Ephesians 2:19.

WE SUFFER TODAY from political projects disguised as moral issues. Trying to create a neighborhood without a brotherhood is frustrating business. The only true brotherhood is the fellowship of twice-born believers in Jesus Christ. It does not segregate itself into isolated Utopias as has been tried many times. Paul made that clear in 1 Corinthians 5:9,10. It is a spiritual fellowship in this world but not of it. Our home is not here but in the hereafter. We are strangers and pilgrims in this world of the once-born. Pagan Paradises come to naught trying to make brothers of men who are only neighbors with unchanged hearts. The saints may not have a community but they have communion!

BONES, BODY, BREATH

Prophesy upon these bones, and say unto them, O ye dry bones, hear the word of the Lord. Ezekiel 37:4.

EZEKIEL'S VISION OF the valley of dry bones sets before us bones, body, and breath. It is possible to have the bones of theological truth, a body of moral character, but without the breath of the Spirit one is still a lost soul. A church may have a fine skeleton of organization, the body of a large membership and yet without the breath of God be only a Sardis having a name to be alive but dead. A mortician can make a dead man look better than he ever looked when he was alive! How the bones and body of professing Christianity need the wind of the Spirit to blow upon them! How we need to pray as well as to sing, "Holy Spirit, breathe on me"!

APRIL 15

DON'T FENCE GOD IN!

For ever, O Lord, thy word is settled in heaven.   Psalms 119:89.
*Oh that thou wouldest rend the heavens, that thou wouldest come
down. . . .   Isaiah 64:1.*

GOD HAS ORDAINED fixed physical and moral laws in the universe.
We cannot really break them but we can break ourselves against them.
God is not mocked and what we sow we shall reap. But these laws
are not an ironclad set of rules that limit God Himself. He is not the
prisoner of His own laws. When He so wills and the situation calls
for it, He does not break but transcends His laws in ways not contranatural but supernatural. God has not fenced Himself in!

APRIL 16

NOT FAR TO HEAVEN

To day shalt thou be with me in paradise.   Luke 23:43.

WE STOOD IN the Smokies in mid-October viewing the matchless
autumn glory. One of our group said, "It just can't be far from here
to heaven." It is never far to heaven if your life is hid with Christ in
God—only a couple of breaths away from the hereafter! Look not at
some distant star and fancy your homeland lies somewhere beyond
even there. We have not been told much about how near or far that
celestial host may be. They may be nearer than we think! At any rate,
it can't be long until He comes or we go! We are not far from heaven.

APRIL 17

ALL CAME TO PASS

There failed not ought. . . .   Joshua 21:45.

WE WORRY AND doubt and fear, grow impatient and rebellious. Then we look back across the years and discern that all the while God was weaving a pattern where all things worked together for good. I remember now a time long ago when I could have said with Jacob, "All these things are against me." In one of my darkest hours, I had to turn my course and abandon old plans for new, to find that behind the dim unknown God stood within the shadow keeping watch above His own. "All came to pass," says the verse in Joshua. And so say I!

APRIL 18

THE JUDAS KISS

[Judas] came to Jesus and said, Hail, Master; and kissed him.
Matthew 26:49.

JUDAS BETRAYED THE Lord with a kiss, not with a slap. More people betray Him with a show of affection than any other way. They call Him, Lord, and do not what He says. "They profess that they know God; but in works they deny him, being abominable, and disobedient, and unto every good work reprobate" (Titus 1:16). They sit in church and sing His praises and outwardly confess Him. They call Him Master and kiss Him. Many a hymn sung and a creed recited is but a Judas kiss. A slap would be more honest!

APRIL 19

REDEEMED!

Your redemption draweth nigh. . . . Luke 21:28.

REDEMPTION FROM SIN has been accomplished already. All who avail themselves of what was wrought on Calvary have been bought in the market, bought out of the market, never again to be on sale in the market. The redemption of our bodies awaits the resurrection when all who have been redeemed through faith in Christ shall be transformed and take their new bodies fashioned like His glorious body. Then follows the redemption of all creation. When the saints rule on an earth set free from the blight of decay and death, man and beast will be at peace. God has set His face to redeem man and nature from the havoc wrought by the devil. "Lift up your heads; for your redemption draweth nigh!"

APRIL 20

STUBBORNNESS

Stubbornness is as iniquity and idolatry. 1 Samuel 15:23.

FROM GILGAL TO Gilboa, the story of King Saul may be summed up in one word, *stubbornness.* We do not classify stubbornness with iniquity and idolatry, but God does. We are told, "Be ye not . . . as the mule" (Psalms 32:9) whose outstanding characteristic is stubbornness, always backward about going forward. Saul had many admirable points but he never learned that "to obey is better than sacrifice." There was a New Testament Saul who started out as stubborn as the Old Testament Saul, but one day on the Damascus Road Jesus Christ met him and he took the road of submission to find victory through surrender.

Is yours the Gilboa Road or the Damascus Road?

NOT REVIVAL BUT "VIVAL"

But grow in grace, and in the knowledge of our Lord and Saviour Jesus Christ. 2 Peter 3:18.

EVERYWHERE WE SEE signs advertising "Revivals." Preachers speak of "holding" revivals . . . somebody ought to turn one loose! But actually God never intended that revival should be the norm—periodic backsliding and repenting. The Christian life was meant to be perennial, not seasonal with spring and summer followed by fall and winter. We have come to think of revivals as necessary and they are as things now stand, but they were never meant to be. Normal New Testament Christianity is "vival" that does not need constant rekindling. The "malarial" brand—fever followed by chills—is subnormal and abnormal.

APRIL 22

EITHER/OR

He that is not with me is against me; and he that gathereth not with me scattereth abroad. Matthew 12:30.

HERE IS A great evangelism text and I marvel that I have never heard it used in that connection. It allows for only two kinds of people. It is not relative but absolute. We divide humanity horizontally, high class, middle class, low class. God divides vertically, to the right and to the left. This cuts against the grain of popular thinking. They say that there are so many grades, shades, degrees, varieties of people, they cannot be lumped arbitrarily into lost and saved, for Christ or against Christ. But Christ leaves no neutral ground, no middle way. He does not recognize *neither nor.* With Him, we are *either or.*

APRIL 23

MAKING LIGHT OF IT

But they made light of it. . . . Matthew 22:5.

THE INVITATION TO the king's wedding did not fall on hostile ears, just indifferent ears, except for a few. The greatest hindrance to the Gospel and all the efforts of the Church is found in those who do not take it seriously, who even joke about it. My heart has been chilled to hear the facetious remarks, the wisecracks that church members often make concerning revival or the preacher's message. Outright scorn and bitter opposition are easier to cope with than the careless, superficial disregard of those who merely go their way as though the concerns of the soul were secondary. The Wedding Feast of the King's Son is nothing to joke about lightly!

APRIL 24

YOU MUST DECIDE

Choose you this day whom ye will serve. . . . Joshua 24:15.

IT IS ALL very well to say the Lord will work things out, but we cannot pass the buck of final decision. He may give leadings, set up circumstances, urge us within, open doors, but we must say *yes* or *no*. Throughout the Book, He says, "Come, follow, drink, confess, turn, repent." "If any man hear my voice" is not enough, he must open the door. The Prodigal Son said, "I will arise and go to my father," and we read next that he arose and went. Resolution must be followed by action. God invested us with the awesome power of choice. Otherwise we would be robots. Neither God nor anyone else can decide for us. The privilege involves possibilities beyond all reckoning for good or evil, heaven or hell. And never forget that not to choose the right is to accept the wrong. We do not make up our minds to miss the will of God and go to hell—that will happen eventually anyhow if we do not choose God's will and heaven.

APRIL 25

SURVIVING SAINTS

I only, am left. . . . I have left me seven thousand. . . .
1 Kings 19:10,18.

ELIJAH IN THE cave thought he was the surviving saint, the only good man left. God corrected him for his statistics were all wrong. Seven thousand remained who had not bowed to Baal. The old Straight and Narrow is not crowded, few there be who travel it, but you are not the only pilgrim. Let no Elijah bemoan his solitary state as a lone survivor. God has more faithful left than we think.

APRIL 26

TOUCHERS NOT THRONGERS

Thou seest . . . sayest thou, who touched me? Mark 5:31.

OUR LORD SAW the crowd, but what concerned Him most was the woman who touched Him. Crowds at church on Sunday may be impressive, but more important are not the *throngers* but the *touchers.* He is looking for that desperate soul who gets through the pressing multitude and makes contact. She did not look very important, dying with a terminal illness, penniless, health gone, money gone, but faith not gone. Our Lord asked for a public confession, a testimony "before all the people." What is needed most today is not a multitude of *throngers* but *touchers* who witness to the miracle of His power.

APRIL 27

LEST I MYSELF BE A CASTAWAY

But I keep under my body, and bring it into subjection: lest that by any means, when I have preached to others, I myself should be a castaway. 1 Corinthians 9:27.

PAUL LIVED BY rigid discipline, took no chances, was not shadowboxing but running the race in dead earnest, lest he be disapproved. God's servant is never safe from falling until he gets home. He gives God the benefit of every doubt, follows the rule "When in doubt, don't!" He denies himself things that may not be evil but may make it easier to sin. He makes no provision for the flesh and avoids what might not be dangerous for others but holds a built-in snare for him. A workman approved unto God, not a castaway disapproved!

APRIL 28

FAITH WITHOUT WORKS

They profess that they know God; but in works they deny him....
Titus 1:16.

MOST CHURCH MEMBERS have worked out a clever system by which they profess to be Christians without becoming involved in the implications of that name. They claim Jesus as Saviour but deny Him as Lord. They want the privileges without the obligations. On Sunday morning they sing, "To the old rugged cross I will ever be true, its shame and reproach gladly bear," but they never go to Christ's camp bearing His reproach. If even half of our church membership ever took Jesus Christ seriously, it would start a major revolution! "Faith without works is dead."

APRIL 29

THE STAY-AT-HOMES

Why abodest thou among the sheepfolds, to hear the bleatings of the flocks? Judges 5:16.

THE REUBENITES HAD "great thoughts of heart," but, although they appeared patriotic, they stayed at home in the peaceful security of the pastures, piping on their handmade reedy flutes while other tribes went to battle. Like Meroz, they came not to the help of the Lord against the mighty. We have them in abundance in the Church today, good soldiers in a dress parade when the bugles are blowing and the drums are beating and the flags are waving, but, when real conflict with evil breaks out, they abide among the sheepfolds. They often wear the finest uniforms who never go to war!

APRIL 30

YES OR NO

But let your communication be, Yea, yea; Nay, nay: for whatsoever is more than these cometh of evil.   Matthew 5:37.

WE CANNOT BE *neither/nor* in a world where the real issues are *either/or*. Jesus recognized no middle ground, no neutral territory: "He that is not with me is against me; and he that gathereth not with me scattereth abroad" (Matthew 12:30). There are, to use the words of Joseph Parker, "no graded lines, light compounded with shadow in a graceful exercise of give and take." It is up or down, in or out, saved or lost, heaven or hell. Anything more than that is of the devil.

MAY 1

EXILES FROM EDEN

Therefore the Lord God sent him forth from the garden of Eden. . . .   Genesis 3:23.

GOD PUT ADAM and Eve in Eden and, if they had behaved themselves, they might have lived in peace and plenty. But Satan entered, man fell, and God drove our first parents from their first home. Humanity has been trying to return home ever since. The Bible is God's record of man's heartbreaking journey in search of his lost estate. It begins with Paradise lost and ends with Paradise regained.

We are exiles from Eden and all Christians are pilgrims to Paradise, to the River of Life and the Tree of Life in their final and eternal abode. Jesus had no earthly home, but He is the Way to the Father's House and its many mansions. If we trust and obey Him, we are on our way home!

MAY 2

GRACE FOR ALL GEARS

But they that wait upon the Lord shall renew their strength; they shall mount up with wings as eagles; they shall run, and not be weary; and they shall walk, and not faint.   Isaiah 40:31.

IN LIFE THE gears shift in reverse, high, intermediate, and low, as we move from youth through middle age into senior citizenship. But there is grace for all *gears* and our verse presents flying grace, running grace, walking grace. There is this blessed difference from the usual course of things: even in old age, although God does not turn time backward in its flight, our youth may be renewed as the eagle's (Psalms 103:5), a new lease on life for the last chapter!

MAY 3

FAITHFUL IN THE LEAST

He that is faithful in that which is least is faithful also in much. . . .   Luke 16:10.

IN THIS DAY of internationalism, patriotism is at low ebb. A man is a better world citizen if he is faithful to his own country. He is a better member of the human family at large if he is true to his own family. Some are so *universal* that they are of little *local* use. Some claim to belong to the universal Church who are not active in any local church. They remind us of the man who wanted to join a church choir but would not join the church. His argument was that he belonged to the invisible church. The pastor of the local church he would not join suggested that he join the invisible choir!

MAY 4

NOT ISOLATION BUT INSULATION

He that is begotten of God keepeth himself, and that wicked one toucheth him not. 1 John 5:18.

THE CHRISTIAN DOES not isolate himself from a needy world. The salt of the earth must be rubbed into the decay and misery of humanity, but he can be insulated against the contagion, the evil, he encounters everywhere. One would be foolish to shut himself up in a house for fear of germs outside. Let him rather develop his health until he is immunized against the microbes. So may a healthy Christian move uncontaminated among men of iniquity. Of course, it is Christ who keeps him as he abides in Him.

MAY 5

UNTIL AND UNTO

Be thou faithful unto death, and I will give thee a crown of life. Revelation 2:10.

WHILE IN SCRIPTURE the same word may indicate *until* or *unto,* there is a difference between being faithful until we die and being faithful to the dying point, willing to die for what we believe. We read of those who loved not their lives unto the death (Revelation 12:11). They were willing to make the supreme sacrifice. It would be interesting to know how many modern Americans would die for their country and how many Christians would die for their faith.

MAY 6

THINK IT NOT STRANGE

Beloved, think it not strange concerning the fiery trial which is to try you, as though some strange thing happened unto you: But rejoice, inasmuch as ye are partakers of Christ's sufferings; that, when his glory shall be revealed, ye may be glad also with exceeding joy. 1 Peter 4:12,13.

WHEN DISASTER, BEREAVEMENT, persecution, testings come our way, *think it not strange.* How tempted we are to ask, "Why did it have to happen to me?" We wonder what we did or didn't do to bring down this calamity on our heads. We are utterly bewildered; there seems no sense to it; it appears that heaven is brass and God is looking the other way. We are not only bidden to think it not strange *but to rejoice!* If we even managed the negative, how on earth can we be happy at a time like this! But we can and it is the duty and privilege of all the beloved to master both lessons in this course and come out singing. "Think it not strange . . . But rejoice!"

MAY 7

THE GOD-BREATHED BOOK

All scripture is given by inspiration of God. . . . 2 Timothy 3:16.

WE DO NOT worship the Bible for that would be bibliolatry, but it is the only authorized textbook of our faith. Jesus said, "The words that I speak unto you, they are spirit, and they are life" and those words are recorded only in the Bible. The Book is God-breathed and when we explore that Book we feel, as Dr. J. B. Phillips puts it, like one wiring an old house where the power has not been cut off. Some get a charge, some a shock, for it is wired from heaven!

MAY 8

EVERY HILL SHALL BE MADE LOW

And Solomon loved the Lord. . . . only he sacrificed and burnt incense in high places. 1 Kings 3:3.

SOLOMON SET THE pace as it were and, throughout the record of the Kings, these places of idolatry were never abolished. Even in times of great reformation somehow there was this glaring exception, but "the high places." Many a life marked by great improvements and religious activity is marred by a high place, a god and an altar that have never been destroyed. The lowest place in many a record is *the high place!* Is there a secret shrine in your life where you bow to another god than the Lord? As with Solomon, it may have begun innocently enough, but the end is idolatry.

MAY 9

NO MIRACLE BUT. . . .

John did no miracle: but all things that John spake of this man were true. And many believed on him there. John 10:41,42.

JOHN THE BAPTIST did not heal the sick, raise the dead, feed the multitude, but his witness to Jesus Christ was true and, when the Saviour came along, He was recognized as the original. God has not called us to be showmen, do spectacular wonders, and thrill a sensation-crazy generation. He has ordained us to be faithful by life and lip to His Christ and when we do, men will believe on Him. At the Last Day, the greatest rewards may go to unknown witnesses whose lives were a day-by-day testimony in the common walks of life. More disciples are won by them than by all the celebrities! John was something of both, but it was his message and not miracles that won others to Christ. No miracle but . . . !

MAY 10

WAITING AND WATCHING

And what I say unto you I say unto all, Watch.   Mark 13:37.

WE ARE ALL waiting for the Lord's return. We have to wait since we cannot hurry it up. But waiting is not watching. Some say, "I am not interested in prophecy. Nobody knows the time and all we can do is to be ready." But the early Christians were not only ready, they lived in expectancy. Blessed is that servant whom his Lord will find not only ready but watching. His eyes are on the Eastern skies—more ways than one!—for his redemption draws nigh. I am concerned about those who say nonchalantly, "Oh, *of course* I believe the Lord is coming back." It is not a matter *of course!* We are to be busy and occupy ourselves till He comes, but we labor in joyful anticipation. We not only wait, we watch!

MAY 11

NO PROPHET FROM GALILEE

Out of Galilee ariseth no prophet.   John 7:52.

SO SAID THE people and so said the enemies of Jesus. The Establishment at Jerusalem, the dignitaries and aristocrats at the capital despised the ruralites in Galilee. Must not prophets come from the higher echelons? They were wrong and should have known it from past history. Jonah, Hosea, Nahum, perhaps even Elijah, Elisha, Amos came from Galilee. God brought His Son from such background, and He usually does the same thing today. We read that the meeting broke up and everybody went home except Jesus who had no home and went to the Mount of Olives. The picture does not change even today!

MAY 12

RAT RACE

He hath sent me . . . to preach deliverance to the captives. . . .
Luke 4:18.

IN A PET shop today, I saw a small rat in a plastic ball trying to get out, of course, but only rolling all over the place. It was a perfect picture of humanity today imprisoned in its own gadgets going all directions making what some call progress but still imprisoned. Unlike the rat, we have devised our own plastic ball, painted ourselves into a corner, built our own jail, forged our own chains, and the more we try to throw them off the more tightly bound we become.

There is One who came long ago to set the captives free. If we continue in His Word then are we His disciples; we shall know the Truth and the Truth shall set us free.

MAY 13

WALLED AROUND BUT NOT ROOFED OVER

Neither know we what to do: but our eyes are upon thee.
2 Chronicles 20:12.

JEHOSHAPHAT WAS COMPASSED about but not covered for the uplook was good. When Elisha was surrounded by the enemy, he looked up to behold the angels of the Lord encamping round about him from above. Satan can wall us around, but he cannot roof us over. When Isaiah looked back at the past and around at the present, he found hope in the upward look: "Oh that thou wouldest rend the heavens, that thou wouldest come down" (Isaiah 64:1). Circumstances may limit our outreach but not our upreach. Keep looking up!

MAY 14

THE THINNING VEIL

Then shall I know. . . .   1 Corinthians 13:12.

THE OTHER DAY I came across this precious word from G. Campbell Morgan: "The veil that divides us from the life on the other side seems to grow thinner as our dear ones pass within it." Down here, when a dear one moves to another part of the country, that country takes on new meaning and our interest in it grows. With some of us, most of our family has moved and the population has shifted. Heaven is no longer remote, far, far away. There is a new affinity, a precious communion with another world. Not communication, but a sense of nearness, as though now we were near the border line. The veil grows thinner and we can hardly wait until it disappears! As a little boy I read *Through the Looking Glass,* and wished I could get through our old mirror into that strange land! A feeling something like that grips me now as I see through a glass darkly and wonder how it will be beyond.

MAY 15

YET BELIEVING

Blessed are they that have not seen, and yet have believed.   John 20:29. *Whom having not seen, ye love; in whom, though now ye see him not, yet believing, ye rejoice with joy unspeakable and full of glory. . . .*   1 Peter 1:8.

THOMAS WANTED TO see and touch, the evidence of the senses, and so wanted a smaller blessing than he already had in believing without seeing. Here seeing is not believing, but believing is seeing. Today men must see, so even the Church puts on shows; men must feel, so we have gone on an emotional binge. Blessed are they who may not see or feel but believe anyway!

MAY 16

DARKNESS AND DAWN

Now from the sixth hour there was darkness over all the land unto the ninth hour. Matthew 27:45. *In the end of the sabbath, as it began to dawn. . . .* Matthew 28:1.

OUR LORD DIED in the dark and rose with the dawn. The darkness was in the daytime, a strange miracle, the blackest period of all time when sin was dealt with once and for all and my Lord cried, "My God, my God, why hast thou forsaken me?". It was as though nature herself could not bear the awfulness of those moments that assured one day her total redemption. But dawn follows darkness and never so truly as on the Resurrection morning. With it comes the blessed assurance that all saints who died in darkness however dark will one day rise in eternal dawn. If darkness comes, can dawn be far behind?

MAY 17

REAFFIRMATION

These things I will that thou affirm constantly. . . . Titus 3:8.

WE ARE BORN only once into this world and we are born only once into the Kingdom of God. There is no need to be reborn after being born again. There should be a once-for-all dedication of all we are and have, which should take place when we are born again. But sometimes faith flags and trouble besets us and days are dark and health fails and we do well to reaffirm our faith. There is all the difference in the world between this and getting converted again and again as some poor souls do until it becomes a habit. Affirm it and act upon it and you will find that it grows by exercise.

74

MAY 18

LONESOME VALLEY

Yea, though I walk through the valley . . . thou art with me. . . .
Psalms 23:4.

I LOVE THE old folk melody that says: "You must walk that lonesome valley, you must walk it by yourself; nobody else can walk it for you, you must walk it by yourself." But it begins by saying that Jesus walked His Lonesome Valley and it comes to a victorious finish by affirming that He is walking by our side. Not even He can walk that valley *for* us, but He can walk it *with* us. He assured us, "Lo, I am with you alway, even unto the end of the world." No one, not even the Lord, can assume our responsibility to walk our valley, but sometimes precious human companionship helps make it less lonely and our Lord will never leave us nor forsake us. Lonesome Valley! He doesn't walk it *for* us, but He does walk it *with* us!

MAY 19

CATCH UP WITH THE FLAG!

To me to live is Christ. . . .   Philippians 1:21.

I HAVE READ of a battle where the flag bearers got far ahead of the troops. Someone called back, "Shall we bring the flag back to the regiment?" The Captain answered, "No, the regiment must catch up with the flag!" The Christian standard has been brought back to the low living of most of our church members. It is high time we catch up with what we stand for, change our way of living or change our name. "To live is Christ," that is our flag, our ideal, our standard. Any retreat from it spells defeat.

MAY 20

MARRED

The vessel . . . was marred. . . . Jeremiah 18:4. *His visage was so marred. . . .* Isaiah 52:14.

ALL CREATION LIES marred today in the bondage of corruption because of sin. Lives are wrecked and hearts are broken by the power of evil. Our bodies are distorted and disfigured by disease. Some of us have watched our dearest pass away scarcely recognizable. Is there an answer? Yes, the dying Saviour was so marred that He did not look like a man—and all so that marred sinners might be saved, that marred bodies might be changed into the likeness of our Lord's glorious Resurrection body, that all creation might be restored to its original loveliness. He was marred that we might never be marred again!

MAY 21

DO YOU HAVE THE RIGHT TIME?

Many years . . . this night. . . . Luke 12:19,20.

THE FOOLISH FARMER would fill his barns and then say to his soul, "Take it easy—you are well fixed for many years." But God said, "You fool, not many years but *this night* is the correct time!" It is well to set our timepiece with God's clock. There is a lot of difference between *many years* and *this night*. We have Daylight Saving Time, but there is another far more important Soul Saving Time: "Behold, now is the accepted time; behold, now is the day of salvation" (2 Corinthians 6:2). Today is God's time. Tonight your soul may be required. Set your watch with heaven and not the faulty timepieces of earth. Do you have the correct time?

MAY 22

THREE WAYS TO GET A MEAL

Give us this day our daily bread.   Matthew 6:11.

THERE ARE SEVERAL ways to get a meal. You can prepare it yourself. You can go down a cafeteria line and take what you wish. You can sit in a restaurant and wait until it is brought to you. We need not ask God to do for us those things we can do ourselves by His Spirit. Other blessings are ours for the taking, anytime, always available. Some things we must ask for and wait until they come. Some things are not provided because they are not good for us and God knows what is best for His children. A man who waited in a restaurant for his breakfast finally went away leaving on the table a note that read, "Out for lunch"! Some of us grow weary waiting. We should distinguish between what we must wait for, what we may take, and what we must provide for ourselves.

MAY 23

LOOKING AND SEEING

Look unto me, and be ye saved, all the ends of the earth. . . .
Isaiah 45:22.

GOD PROMISED THAT all who looked upon the fiery serpent in the wilderness should live (Numbers 21:8). Jesus said that is the way we are saved, not by seeing but by looking. I do not think the Israelites on the back row of all that multitude could see the serpent very well, but they could look. Alexander Whyte advised a troubled soul: "He does not say, 'See': He only says 'Look.' " We do not have to comprehend or understand salvation. A course in theology is not required. Just, "Look . . . and be ye saved."

MAY 24

A WORD FOR THE WEARY

The Lord God hath given me the tongue of the learned, that I should know how to speak a word in season to him that is weary. . . .   Isaiah 50:4.

THIS MESSIANIC PRONOUNCEMENT by our Lord can also be our experience. He proclaimed His mission to the brokenhearted—prophesied in Isaiah and fulfilled in Luke. The language of heartbreak is not learned in the schools of men but in the furnace of suffering and the crucible of trouble. The tuition comes high, but the rewards are precious in hearts comforted, fears dispelled, faith renewed. The speech of the bereaved is not a collection of nice platitudes by people who have never "been there." He who becomes a brother to the bruised, a doctor of the despairing, a comforter to the crushed may not actually say much. What he has to offer is often beyond the power of speech to convey. But the weary sense it and it is balm of Gilead to the soul. Have you found words in season for him that is weary?

MAY 25

THE PATIENCE OF UNANSWERED PRAYER

Call unto me, and I will answer thee. . . .   Jeremiah 33:3.

SOMETIMES THE ANSWER is long delayed. When Mary and Martha sent word to Jesus that Lazarus was sick, He abode two days still in the place where He was. It must have been exasperating to the sisters and they complained later about it. Sometimes we get the opposite of what we pray for. Paul did not get his request for the removal of his thorn in the flesh but more grace instead. Prayer may not get us what we want, but it will teach us to want what we need. Better learn to pray with George Croly's great hymn for "the patience of unanswered prayer."

TRUSTING JESUS, THAT IS ALL

His heart is fixed, trusting in the Lord.   Psalms 112:7.

WE MAKE FAITH more difficult than God ever made it. We exercise faith a hundred times a day in just about everything we do, but, when it comes to believing God, we make a mighty mystery out of it and fence it about with difficulties that make it well-nigh impossible. Sure, it is the gift of God, but it comes by hearing and hearing by the Word of God. God says it and we simply take Him at His Word. If it were as complicated as we have made it to be, most poor souls would never make it. Indeed, it is the simple heart that grasps it while scholars miss it. God has kept it from the wise and prudent and revealed it unto babes. Just trusting Jesus, *that is all.* Unless we become as little children and stop trying to be theologians who sometimes see it last, we shall never have fixed hearts like the Psalmist wrote about but only feverish heads.

A STORY TO TELL TO THE NEIGHBORS

Beginning at Jerusalem.   Luke 24:47.

BEFORE OUR GOSPELIZING gets around to the uttermost part of the earth, it should begin at home, "in Jerusalem" as it were. We have a story to tell to the nations, but it is also a story to tell to the neighbors all around us. It is easier to send money across the sea to tell it to the heathen than to send *me* across the street to tell it to people I know. It is a poor light that is made to shine brighter in the distance than close at hand. Too many are missionaries by proxy but not in person. God's program begins where we live.

MAY 28

FAITH IN CHRIST IS NOT A GAMBLE

For ever, O Lord, thy word is settled in heaven.   Psalms 119:89.

OCCASIONALLY SOMEBODY TALKS about staking everything on faith in Jesus Christ, as though it were a gamble. A gamble is a risk on something that may or may not be true, something that may happen or may not happen, something or someone that may or may not be dependable. We are not taking any risks when we step out on the Word of God. Forever it is firm, fixed, final, tried, and true. We may seem to be stepping out in an empty void but underneath is the Rock of Ages. Strange indeed that the idea ever got around that we are taking a chance with the Changeless! How firm a foundation is laid for our faith in His excellent Word!

MAY 29

STATUTES AND SONGS

Thy statutes have been my songs in the house of my pilgrimage.
Psalms 119:54.

A POSTGRADUATE STUDENT, studying cello under Pablo Casals, played his number in a way that seemed to us excellent, but the great maestro said, "You are playing the notes but not the music!" The Church today numbers one category of Christians whose spiritual experience is wild music without the notes of sound doctrine, a lot of noise that needs a tune. On the other hand, there are thousands who have the notes correct theologically, but there is no melody, no joyous praise, no hallelujah. These two extremes ought to get together, join mandate with melody, and find in God's lawbook a songbook. Then our delight would be in the law of the Lord, service with not merely a smile but a song.

MAY 30

GOD, FATHER OF US AND TO US

Wherefore come out from among them, and be ye separate, saith
the Lord, and touch not the unclean thing; and I will receive you,
And will be a Father unto you, and ye shall be my sons and
daughters, saith the Lord Almighty. 2 Corinthians 6:17,18.

DOES THE FATHERHOOD of God depend on separation? No, it depends on regeneration. We become God's children by being born again. But God cannot be the Father *to* us that He wants to be when we are in fellowship with evil. Many earthly fathers cannot be the fathers to their sons they want to be because the rebellion and habits of that son make it impossible. God could do infinitely more for some of us than we allow Him to do. He may be the Father *of* us but cannot be a Father *to* us. Are you enjoying His fellowship that grows out of His relationship but is hindered by our fellowship with unrighteousness, our communion with darkness, our concord with Belial?

MAY 31

WINDOWS IN HEAVEN

If the Lord would make windows in heaven, might this thing be?
2 Kings 7:2. *Prove me now herewith, saith the Lord of hosts, if I*
will not open you the windows of heaven, and pour you out a
blessing, that there shall not be room enough to receive it.
Malachi 3:10.

THE CYNIC ASKED Elisha in unbelief, "Might this thing be?" Famine was raging and relief by tomorrow seemed preposterous, but it came. God challenges us to prove Him in our giving. We cannot outgive God. Heaven's windows are ready to open today, but our unbelief and our witholding from God keep the skies brazen. "O that Thou would-est rend the heavens and come down!" When we rend our hearts and not our garments, He will rend the heavens.

JUNE 1

THE DOUBLE DEPOSIT

He is able to keep that which I have committed [*my deposit*] *unto him against that day.* 2 Timothy 1:12. *That good thing which was committed unto thee keep by the Holy Ghost which dwelleth in us.* 2 Timothy 1:14.

IT IS NOT enough to have faith in the bank, we must make the deposit. Paul had deposited everything, all he was and had, to God to keep. God keeps all we deposit with Him until the Judgment Day. If it is safe that long, rest assured it will be safe from there on! On the other hand, God has given us a charge to keep, a treasure in earthen vessels.

> Have we been true to the trust He left us?
> Do we seek to do our best?
> If in our hearts there is naught condemns us,
> We shall have a glorious rest.
>
> FANNY J. CROSBY

JUNE 2

ROYAL ROBES AND SACKCLOTH

He [*King Joram*] *had sackcloth within upon his flesh.*
2 Kings 6:30.

KING JORAM WORE his royal robes without, but, in this hour of dire national calamity, he wore at least the emblem of repentance within. Today the world wears the gay garments of outward popularity and success, but never has humanity had such need to don sackcloth as now. National leaders boast that we can handle our troubles and even churchmen brag of our competence to meet the crisis. When will we hear the prophet, "Lie all night in sackcloth, ye ministers of my God . . ."? Never has there been more gayety without and more misery within, but there is lacking the broken and contrite heart which God will not despise.

JUNE 3

HOW TEDIOUS AND TASTELESS

Why art thou cast down, O my soul?   Psalms 42:11; 43:5.

SHALLOW SOULS WHO have never known much sorrow grow almost irritated with John Newton sighing, "Why do I languish and pine?" and praying, "Drive these dark clouds from my sky" and "take me . . . where winter and clouds are no more." But all who have companioned with trouble and walked the dark valley find a kinship not only with Newton but with David and Jeremiah and Paul and many another who at times hung their harps on the willows. For the believing soul, December should indeed be as pleasant as May, but there are times when even May can be dreary. Faith goes ahead anyway not doubting the sun because the clouds obscure it, believing God anyway, assured that, with the Psalmist who wrote our text, we shall yet praise Him who is the health of our countenance and our God.

JUNE 4

WITH

He that is not with me is against me; and he that gathereth not with me scattereth abroad.   Matthew 12:30.

MAKE SURE THAT you are not just *for* Christ but first of all *with* Him; your life hid *with* Christ in God. Without Him, you can do nothing. Then, when death comes, you depart to be *with* Him which is far better (Philippians 1:21). When He returns, all who sleep in Jesus He will bring *with* Him. We who remain shall be caught up together *with* them to meet the Lord in the air and so shall we ever be *with* the Lord (1 Thessalonians 4:14–17). "With them—with Him!" Our Lord said to the penitent thief, "To day shalt thou be with me in paradise." Blessed *withness!* Make sure of it here and hereafter!

JUNE 5

THE MIRROR AND THE WINDOW

Then said I, Woe is me! Whom shall I send, and who will go for us?   Isaiah 6:5,8.

EVERY HEART SHOULD have its mirror and window. God's Word is the divine looking glass that shows us ourselves as we really are (James 1:22–25). After we have looked into it and taken appropriate action, then we are ready to look out the window at a needy world and hear God's call to service in it. Too many are being exhorted to say "Here am I" as Isaiah did before they have ever said "Woe is me!" We have not seen the King, the Lord of hosts. The vision must precede the venture. A look in the mirror comes before the look out the window.

JUNE 6

ETERNITY NOW

While we look not at the things which are seen, but at the things which are not seen: for the things which are seen are temporal; but the things which are not seen are eternal.   2 Corinthians 4:18.

PEOPLE GENERALLY ARE occupied with the things of this world with only an occasional thought about the unseen world beyond. Yet we are surrounded by eternity. Only a step, a heartbeat, a few breaths lie between us and the next and everlasting stage of our existence. For the Christian, eternal life does not begin at death or the Judgment. It began when he trusted Christ. He has already begun it. How we should move through what little time is left as citizens of that next world and pilgrims here! With eternity's values in mind, we ought to walk as foreigners here and natives there. That is our true habitat and our conduct should indicate our homeland.

JUNE 7

BETTER THAN THIS

With Christ; which is far better. . . .   Philippians 1:23.

BEREAVED ONES WHO have lost their dearest ask, "We were so happy. Will that special relationship be continued in heaven? I know the marriage state does not continue, but my dear one will not be just like anyone else it seems to me." I think you are right. Over there everything will be far better and a precious fellowship of spirit between man and wife will not be terminated but perfected. Our Father can be trusted to make everything better than it was here. If both are in Christ, you may be sure our Father will perfect that which concerneth us. If it was that good here, it will be better there!

JUNE 8

EN-CHRISTED

Christ liveth in me. . . .   Galatians 2:20.

STRICTLY SPEAKING, THERE is only one Christian life and that is Christ Himself, but He lives it again and again in all who receive Him. The Christian is en-Christed and what possibilities that suggests! We all have received His fullness—His wisdom, His health, His love, His power—all of these are released in us according to His Word, His will, our need, and our faith. We are still personalities, not robots, and, to the extent that we trust and obey, we may have all we need to do His will as long as He wants us to do it. Some want more than is His will and many live with far less than they might have. Make it your prayer and pursuit that Christ may live in you to the fullest extent of His purpose for you.

JUNE 9

SAINTS IN THE SHADE

Consider him . . . lest ye be wearied and faint in your minds.
Hebrews 12:3.

ELIJAH UNDER THE juniper, the Disobedient Prophet in 1 Kings 13, Jonah under the gourd vine—God's weary prophets did not fare so well in the shade. Shady rest is no place for tired preachers! The next day after a great day can be a dangerous day. Satan does some of his worst work on exhausted Christians when nerves are frayed and the mind is faint. We may, like Elijah, fancy we are the survivors among the saints. Like the prophet of Jeroboam's day, we may fall prey to subtle temptation. Like Jonah, we may be irritable and out of sorts. It is better to be a Nathaniel under a fig tree or Zacchaeus up a sycamore. Jesus knows when we pray and when we are "up a tree." Keep your eyes on Him lest ye faint and be weary and collapse in the shade!

JUNE 10

THUS FAR

Hitherto hath the Lord helped us.   1 Samuel 7:12.

" 'TIS GRACE THAT brought me safe *thus far.* " This much is certain, dear brother or sister: you have made it thus far. The God of the Hitherto is the God of the Henceforth. Look back across the years and things begin to take shape, and what made no sense at the time now fits into the picture. All the way the Saviour has led you, what have you to ask besides? Can you doubt His tender mercy who through life has been your Guide? You have come thus far. You would not go back for anything. The only way *out* is *on*.

JUNE 11

WHO AT MY DOOR IS STANDING?

Behold, I stand at the door, and knock. . . .   Revelation 3:20.

THE EMMAUS DISCIPLES invited Him in: "Abide with us: for it is toward evening, and the day is far spent" (Luke 24:29). Receive Him as Guest and let Him be Host. Tell Him to make Himself at home— be Himself in your heart—just that. Let Him run the place. I used to read signs in home dining rooms that read, "Christ is the Head of this home, the silent Listener to every conversation, present at every meal." I heard of a family that kept a vacant chair always at the head of the table reserved for the Lord. It helped for it reminded them often of One present though to sight unseen. Does He feel at home in your house? Can He be Himself in you?

JUNE 12

THE THREE CANNOTS

And there went great multitudes with him: and he turned and said unto them. . . .   Luke 14:25.

WHAT FOLLOWED ARE the Three Cannots. If we do not hate loved ones and even our own life, we cannot be His disciples. If we do not bear our cross and come after Him, we cannot be His disciples. If we do not forsake all we have, we cannot be His disciples (vs. 26,27,33). Jesus was becoming popular and it was time to thin out the crowd. We see what happened in Constantine's time when Christianity became the thing and everybody wanted to join the Church. Beware of mixed multitudes such as followed Moses out of Egypt. They crack up when the real test comes (Numbers 11:4–6). So do the superficial believers who have no root in themselves (Matthew 13:20,21). There is need to turn on the multitude now and then and thin them with the Three Cannots!

JUNE 13

YOUR NEED IS YOUR TICKET

I am rich, and increased with goods, and have need of nothing. . . .
Revelation 3:17.

LAODICEA HAD NO sense of need and did not realize its true condition. Here is the tragedy in our smug, comfortable churches today. Others who may feel their need try to make themselves worthy to come to the Saviour.

> Let not conscience make you linger,
> Nor of fitness fondly dream;
> All the fitness He requireth
> Is to feel your need of Him.
>
> JOSEPH HART

Our need is our ticket! Just as we are without one plea except His blood and His bidding, "But that Thy blood was shed for me, and that Thou bidd'st me come to Thee."

All you need is your need. His provision and invitation guarantee the rest. But "if you tarry till you're better, you will never come at all."

JUNE 14

ALL THINGS

Having nothing, and yet possessing all things.
2 Corinthians 6:10.

PAUL HAD SUFFERED the loss of all things, yet he says, "All things are yours" and of course that means all things were his, too. Here is the paradox of having both nothing and everything. We may suffer the actual loss of all things as Paul did or be "as though" we had nothing (1 Corinthians 7:29–31). It amounts to the same thing. In ourselves we have nothing; in Christ we have everything. We may be actually poor or have abundance, yet be poor in spirit. Then we are above the tyranny of things and we triumph over them.

JUNE 15

ME AND MY SHADOW

They brought forth the sick into the streets, and laid them on beds and couches, that at the least the shadow of Peter passing by might overshadow some of them.   Acts 5:15.

I REMEMBER AN old song, "Me and My Shadow." You do have a shadow. It is your influence and it goes where you go and sticks closer than a brother. They cannot be separated—you and your shadow. You are passing by, making your way among men only once. How important that your shadow falls upon others as a blessing, not as a blight! To cast a beneficent shadow, you must walk in the Light. Jesus of Nazareth is still passing by and what a Shadow! In the Old Testament, the Shunammite woman perceived that Elisha was an holy man of God who passed by continually. If I walk with the Lord in the light of His Word, He will make both me and my shadow a benediction.

JUNE 16

GOD'S ECOLOGY

*The whole creation groaneth and travaileth in pain together
until now.*   Romans 8:22.

MAN HAS BECOME alarmed over the pollution and the deterioration
of our environment and *ecology* became a familiar word. God
spelled it out long ago when He called it "the bondage of corruption" wrought by sin and Satan. He has told us furthermore that
all creation will one day be redeemed from the curse when our
Lord reigns here with His people. He will send His angels to clean
up the mess as no modern experts can ever do it (Matthew 13:-
41,42). As with everything else, God has the true ecology.

JUNE 17

PERHAPS TODAY

The Son of man cometh at an hour when ye think not.
Luke 12:40.

SOMETIMES I SEE the little sign, PERHAPS TODAY. It means that today
may be the time our Lord shall return. It may be at dawn or at dark,
midday, or midnight. And we want to be not only waiting but watching. Again, perhaps if He does not come for us, this may be the day
when we go to Him. It may be the day when great tragedy, sorrow,
bereavement will befall us. It may be the most glorious day we ever
knew when heaven opens and God pours out a blessing we have not
room enough to receive. The Bible says, "Sanctify yourselves against
to morrow" (Numbers 11:18). It is also well to be sanctified against
today. Life is a string of surprises, good and bad. God lives in the
Everlasting Now and makes much of Today. It is the only day we
have. Yesterday is gone and "tomorrow's sun may never rise" for us.
Do not live as though He might return tomorrow. Perhaps TODAY!

JUNE 18

NO MORE QUESTIONS

In that day ye shall ask me nothing.   John 16:23.

OUR LORD IS saying to His troubled disciples, "I will come back from the dead and you will see me and it will end all the questions you have just asked among yourselves." So it did (John 20:20) and they went to martyrdom unshaken. Then the Holy Spirit came to answer more questions as He does to this day. When our Lord returns, every question, every problem that has worried us will vanish and every interrogation mark will become an exclamation point! All will disappear in the glory of His presence! No more questions!

JUNE 19

FROM GOLD TO BRASS

[Shishak] took away all the shields of gold which Solomon had made. And king Rehoboam made in their stead brasen shields. . . .
1 Kings 14:26,27.

KING SOLOMON'S VESSELS were made of gold. Silver did not count for much then. But when Shishak stole the golden shields, Rehoboam dropped all the way to brass. He did not even stop at silver! When men disobey God and judgment falls, we fall from gold to brass and substitute the cheap for the costly. Brass shines but it is not gold! When the Church is robbed of her true treasures, how often instead of repenting and saying we will have gold or nothing we settle for brass! It is time we returned to the gold standard!

JUNE 20

WEIGHTS

Let us lay aside every weight. . . .   Hebrews 12:1.

IF WE ARE to run well the Christian race, we must not only "lay aside
. . . the sin which doth so easily beset us"—sin with its clinging folds
—but also "every weight." A weight is not necessarily a sin. It may
be something good which others may allow without harm, but, if it
cuts down our speed, if it impedes our progress, if it hinders us so that
we are as one running a race wearing an overcoat, we had better part
with it. There will be other difficulties aplenty and unavoidable hur-
dles without cumbering ourselves with extra luggage we can do without.

JUNE 21

MAJOR SURGERY

If thy right hand offend thee, cut it off. . . .   Matthew 5:30.

CUTTING OFF A hand, plucking out an eye, that is major surgery. Our
Lord means that we must follow drastic procedures to remove anything that might prevent our entering into life. He said that it is better
to enter into life crippled than to go to hell whole. Such radical
procedure is seldom preached these days and in a very low key if at
all. Consequently, we have the frightful tragedy of those who lose
everything rather than give up anything, losing all to keep a part. To
enter into life at any cost, that is all that matters. Better do it and be
a cripple than miss it and be complete.

JUNE 22

THERE'LL BE A WAY

Enoch walked with God. . . .   Genesis 5:24.

I LIVE, WHEN on the road, in motels most of the time. I like to walk, but motels are made for motorists, not pedestrians, and usually they stand on highways and crowded traffic intersections. Sometimes it has looked to me on arrival that walking would not be possible, but I have never failed to find some way to take a stroll.

If you really want to walk with God, there'll be a way. It may not be ideal, it may lead through a dark valley or over rugged mountain passes, but there'll be a way. An invalid spending life between bed sheets can still walk with God. Paul did it in a Roman prison awaiting execution. It may not be your way or my way, but still in God's way there'll be a road to walk with Him.

JUNE 23

A TWO-WAY GOOD CONSCIENCE

Herein do I exercise myself, to have always a conscience void of offence toward God, and toward men.   Acts 24:16.

WE ARE TO love God and our neighbor. The upward beam of the cross suggests the one, the horizontal beam the other. Paul wanted a good conscience in both directions. This is not sinless perfection, but it means that we can be blameless though not faultless, our hearts not condemning us of willful rebellion against God or wrongs not made right as far as in us lies. What a worthy two-way objective possible to the Spirit-led Christian, but it calls, as Paul makes clear, for "exercise"!

93

JUNE 24

DON'T STEAL THE SHOW!

He must increase, but I must decrease.   John 3:30.

RECENTLY I LISTENED to a musician who played so magnificently that I forgot the performer in the beauty of his performance. He is a great artist who can fade out in the glory of his art. He is a great preacher who can get lost in his message. He is a great Christian in whom Christ is magnified whether by life or by death. I have read of a lamplighter in the old days who went along the street at dusk starting the flame in each of the lamps, fading away in the gathering darkness but leaving the lights he had kindled. So does the true Christian bow out to let Christ take the stage. The friend of the Bridegroom does not steal the show!

JUNE 25

FIGURES OF THE TRUE

The figures of the true. . . .   Hebrews 9:24.

WHETHER IT BE the place "where their worm dieth not, and the fire is not quenched" or gates of pearl and streets of gold, it must be remembered that the reality is either worse or better as the case may be than the figure. If the fire of hell is not literal, it is worse than actual fire, and, if the gates of the Celestial City are not actual gold, they are far finer. Gold and pearl are the best we know and God put the figure as high as our poor limited faculties can comprehend. Hell will be far more terrible and heaven far more glorious than we can now imagine. May the one drive us to repentance and the other to rejoicing!

AS THE ANGELS OF GOD

In the resurrection they neither marry, nor are given in marriage,
but are as the angels of God in heaven.   Matthew 22:30.

IT IS POSSIBLE to read more out of or into this verse than was intended. Our Lord is simply saying, not that we become angels, but
that, as with the angels, the marriage relationship does not obtain in
the next life. Dr. John Albert Broadus says, "There is nothing here
to forbid the persuasion that the relations of earthly life will be
remembered in the future state, the persons recognized, and special
affections cherished with delight." It is unthinkable that the love of
hearts married on earth in the Lord will be ended forever in death.
Love will never lose its own here or hereafter.

KNOWLEDGE AND WISDOM

If any of you lack wisdom, let him ask of God. . . .   James 1:5.

IF YOU LACK knowledge, go to school. If you lack wisdom, get on
your knees! Knowledge is not wisdom. Wisdom is the proper use of
knowledge. One may have loads of learned lumber in his head and not
know what or how to build with it. Wisdom is the gift of God. He
is not stingy. But we must ask in faith, not wavering, for then we are
like tossing waves of the sea, unstable in all our ways. What we ask
for we must believe we receive and we shall have, not hoping but
believing (*see* Mark 11:24; Matthew 21:22).

JUNE 28

BUDGETING OUR TIME

So teach us to number our days, that we may apply our hearts unto wisdom. Psalms 90:12.

THIS DOES NOT mean that we should count our days because we do not know how many we have. But time is priceless and when it is running out we must be all the more careful how we spend what is left. We should budget our time and put it to good use for one day we must report on how we spent it. The Psalmist is asking God for instruction on how to use the time He has entrusted to us. This does not mean that we must live in nervous tension keeping books on every minute. God is not a tyrant or a taskmaster. He is the Father of all who believe. To study, work, and play as His children, we must give proper place to each and buy up all life's opportunities, "redeeming the time."

JUNE 29

NOW THEE ALONE I SEEK

Christ Jesus, my Lord: for whom I have suffered the loss of all things. . . . Philippians 3:8.

DEAR ONES, POSSESSIONS, career, self—do these things mean more to us than Jesus Christ? Is He our supreme love? Do we long to see others in the life to come more than Him? He Himself said we must hate all else if we follow Him. Water that down as you will, you cannot escape the fact that here is a priority most of us have never realized. Sometimes health, finances, dear ones are taken to free us from our crutches and throw us utterly on Him. When He is our Reward, and the Giver means more than His gifts, the Blesser more than His blessings, He will give us whatever else we need, but He must hold the throne of our hearts.

JUNE 30

UP TO NOW

The Lord thy God bare thee . . . until ye came to this place.
Deuteronomy 1:31.

THE SOUL WHO has leaned on Jesus for repose knows, as he looks back over the years that in spite of the mysteries, the miseries, the disappointments, the unanswered questions, the puzzles which he cannot as yet fit into the pattern—in spite of all these—there is a strange awareness that he was being led by a Hand, supported by strength not his own. God's greatness flowed around his incompleteness, 'round his restlessness—God's rest. So many things cannot be accounted for in any other way than to say, "It was the Lord." When we reach the end, we shall find that, all along in ways we knew not, He bare us until we came to this place.

JULY 1

MEMORIES—TREASURES OR TYRANTS?

Forgetting those things which are behind. . . .   Philippians 3:13.
I remember the days of old. . . .   Psalms 143:5.

MEMORIES, WHETHER GOOD or bad, must be handled with care. Bad recollections can drive us to despair. Good remembrances can become idols and lead us to wallow in sentimentality. We can paint the past with glamour it never had and crown dear ones with haloes they never wore. "Distance lends enchantment to the view." Memory can become a tyrant instead of a treasure chest. From the mistakes of the past, let us learn whatever lessons they teach, then forget them, even as God remembers our sins no more. Let precious memories be benedictions but not bonds. Life must be lived and we must get on with the job.

JULY 2

AWAITING THE DAWN

When shall I arise, and the night be gone?   Job 7:4.

THE BIBLE RECORDS many long nights and sleepless saints watching
for the morning (Psalms 130:6). While the world drinks and dances,
souls hard pressed by many a foe ask, "Watchman, what of the
night?" God gives His beloved sleep, but there are times when sleep
gives way to prayer. Our Lord "continued all night in prayer to God"
(Luke 6:12). But though weeping may endure for a night, joy cometh
in the morning (Psalms 30:5), when He shall be as the light of the
morning, even a morning without clouds (2 Samuel 23:4). And, best
of all, we are headed for a city where there shall be no night (Revelation 21:25).

JULY 3

PILGRIMS

Strangers and pilgrims. . . .   1 Peter 2:11.

THE CHRISTIAN IS a citizen of eternity walking through time. He
follows in the footprints of the heroes of faith catalogued in Hebrews
11, also called "strangers and pilgrims." The pilgrim-and-stranger
concept has almost disappeared from a church comfortably settled in
this world. A lot of water has run under the bridge since John Bunyan
wrote *Pilgrim's Progress*. The travelers in that immortal book were
not at home in Vanity Fair. They and those who kept the Fair
seemed barbarians to each other. But lines of demarkation have
been erased until a Christian pilgrim is now viewed as a rare spec-
imen. The Book still calls him a pilgrim and a stranger—". . . let
God be true, but every man a liar . . ." (Romans 3:4)!

JULY 4

ONE OF THESE DAYS

For yet a little while, and he that shall come will come, and will not tarry.   Hebrews 10:37.

DID YOU GET up this morning and from the burnt toast onward you knew that it was going to be "one of those days"? Nothing came out right, that letter you expected did not come, that prayer you prayed was not answered, your arthritis acted up worse than ever and all you were aware of was the cold hard law of cause and effect. Not a break in the clouds, not a hint of heaven, everything was of the earth— earthy. Never mind, dear heart, it may have been "one of those days," but ahead lies "one of these days," another kind of day. If you are in Christ, beyond the snow of winter lies the sunshine of spring, beyond the grave lies resurrection. Yet a little while and He that shall come *will come* and will not tarry. . . .

One of these days.

JULY 5

BACKBONES MUST BEND

Be ye stedfast, unmovable. . . .   1 Corinthians 15:58.

THIS STEDFAST IMMOVABILITY is not like a monument but like a backbone that can be rigid but can also bend. In matters of principle, we should be inflexible. In minor matters where no vital principle is involved, we must be willing to make concessions that do not require compromise. Husbands and wives who would live happily ever after learn early to give and take, to reach agreements by mutual consent. Backbones are indispensable if we are to stand upright, but a man with an unbending backbone is in real trouble. Unmoveable spines lie in graveyards. God made backbones that can bend and also stand rigid. We need to learn to do both to the glory of God.

JULY 6

MAKE YOURSELF AT HOME

Abide with us. . . . Luke 24:29. *Christ liveth in me. . . .*
Galatians 2:20. *I . . . will sup with him. . . .* Revelation 3:20.

SOMETIMES WHEN WE are told in the house of a friend, "Make
yourself at home," they are ill at ease and so are we and nobody is
"at home." Is Jesus "at home" in your heart or are there doors locked
against Him? Is He a welcome guest in your home, indeed the Host
at the head of the table? Does He feel "at home" in some of our
churches? He was outside the door of lukewarm Laodicea. Blessed is
that heart, that home, that church, where the Saviour is not an occasional visitor for special occasions, but a welcome resident who is also
President, where it truly can be said, "Jesus lives here"!

JULY 7

RETURN TRIP

And they rose up the same hour, and returned to Jerusalem. . . .
Luke 24:33.

THE EMMAUS DISCIPLES had already walked seven miles home from
Jerusalem, sad and discouraged, although it was the very day our
Lord had said He would rise from the dead. When He made Himself
known, they rose up *the same hour* and retraced their steps, no
longer sad or weary. It must have been the most exciting seven
miles they ever traveled. Seven miles of sighing became seven
miles of singing! What a host of weary pilgrims need today is a
contact with the living Christ, true to the Scriptures, warming
their hearts, showing up at home, and making happy witnesses of
them all.

JULY 8

THE SPIRE

Lift up your heads. . . . Luke 21:28.

WHEN MY DEAR one lay in her last illness, her room looked out upon a view that included the white steeple of a church in the distance. When someone would start to draw curtains or lower shades, she would say, "Leave the view open, I want to see the church steeple." In her darkest days it spoke of another world and pointed heavenward. As I write these words, I look out a motel window to two church spires and in my loneliness I am reminded of that better world, that eternity to which this poor vale of tears is but an anteroom. I am tired of the cheap attractions these lowlands offer and long to join the "saints above, Who once went sorrowing here! But now they taste unmingled love And joy without a tear."

JULY 9

WE WRESTLE

We wrestle not against flesh and blood, but against principalities, against powers, against the rulers of the darkness of this world, against spiritual wickedness in high places. Ephesians 6:12.

WRESTLING IS PERHAPS the most strenuous of all sports. Every muscle is strained, every nerve is taut, and the shoulders are never more than a few inches from the mat. There is nothing dainty about it. It is not a graceful exercise of give and take. Our Lord wrestled from the temptation to His arrest when He said, ". . . This is your hour and the power of darkness" (Luke 22:53). Paul believed he contended with demonic hosts under the devil. We had better know what we are up against and not underestimate our adversary.

THE IGNORANT MAJORITY

To be conformed to the image of his Son. . . . Romans 8:29.

THE AVERAGE CHURCH member is totally ignorant of the purpose of God in saving us and is no more like Jesus after twenty-five years in the Church than he was when he "joined" it. That he is not only a *being* but also a *becoming,* that God's main business with us is making saints out of sinners, has never crossed his mind. That Christ lives in him and that daily he should be less like himself and more like his Lord is strange doctrine. The few who are growing in grace and in the knowledge of Christ are viewed by the rest with suspicion and sometimes resentment because their godliness shows up the low living of the majority by contrast.

BOOT CAMP

Thou therefore endure hardness as a good soldier of Jesus Christ. 2 Timothy 2:3.

THIS WORLD IS not our home and we lament its sin-wrecked condition, riddled with disease and death and distress. But for the growing of Christian character, it is a proper training ground. If we had no choice of good or evil, we would be robots or manikins, and, if we were in an ideal environment without storm and stress, we would have no foes to face, no trials to endure. You cannot sharpen an axe on a cake of butter. This grindstone we call earth will either dull or sharpen us, either take away or give us an edge. It is a great boot camp for soldiers of the cross and is well equipped to fit us for service above.

JULY 12

JUST A LITTLE WHILE

A little while, and ye shall not see me: and again, a little while,
and ye shall see me. . . . John 16:16.

IT IS OUR Lord's Word to his uneasy disciples and His Word to us
today. It was a sad interval between His death and Resurrection and
the spirits of His followers flagged, but He returned as He said He
would. Today the wait is longer, but beside eternity it is just a little
while. The days have become years and the years have turned into
centuries and the time is not yet. Sorrow, sickness, pain make weary
the hearts of those who wait and watch like those who look through
long nights for the morning. But we have His Word, "Let not your
heart be troubled. . . . [I] will come again" (John 14:27,28).

JULY 13

SHORTLY

Knowing that shortly I must put off this my tabernacle, even as
our Lord Jesus Christ hath shewed me. 2 Peter 1:14.

PETER HAD BEEN told of his approaching death (John 21:18). Every
Christian knows that soon, even at the longest, either the Lord will
come for us or we will go to Him. He should live with that certainty
in the back of his mind in order to keep his perspective straight. There
is but a step between us and death, and eternity borders us ever close
at hand. What a difference that ought to make! We tend to think only
of people with terminal illness in that category, but we are all suffering
from a terminal illness because of what Satan started in Eden. We
must die and our present apparatus is wearing out. We must shortly
put off this tabernacle to await a new outfit when we get our Easter
suits on the Great Getting-Up Morning.

JULY 14

LET GOD TAKE IT OVER

Commit thy way unto the Lord; trust also in him; and he shall bring it to pass. Psalms 37:5.

LOOKING IN AN old Bible today, I find that I had underlined this precious verse nearly forty years ago. Whatever is bugging you, don't try to handle it yourself. There are three stages here: commit it to God; then trust Him day by day to take care of it, and you will find that in His time He works it out. This does not mean you just get rid of it, wash your hands of it, pass the buck. You have a responsibility for there are crosses to bear and every man must carry his own burden, but the Holy Spirit called alongside to help goes His mile while you go your inch. When a pedestrian with a heavy load is picked up by a motorist, he puts his burden down in the car, he does not keep it on his shoulder. The God who can carry you can carry your load. So cast all your care upon Him for He careth for you. If that is His business, let Him do it!

JULY 15

A FIGHT, NOT A FROLIC

If any man will come after me, let him deny himself, and take up his cross, and follow me. Matthew 16:24.

TODAY WE ARE beset by easy ways to do everything: playing the piano becomes a game, mathematics is fun, you can learn without work, become a master of anything without drudgery, become an instant artist, a virtuoso overnight. But our Lord did not call us to a sanctified picnic and a glorified hayride. We do not become saints in our sleep. The old masters of the deeper life found the way straight and narrow with a cross now and a crown hereafter. In *position,* one becomes a saint instantly, but in *condition* the *being* is followed by the *becoming* and that is not fun.

JULY 16

IF WISHES WERE HORSES. . . .

The Lord will perfect that which concerneth me. . . . Psalms
138:8.

"IF WISHES WERE horses, beggars would ride." It is possible to begin
with a fond wish which becomes father to a thought that multiplies
until we have formed a whole philosophy in our wishful thinking. We
must beware of building a doctrine to satisfy our longings. Concerning
the next world, we imagine how things might be and develop theories
that have no proof in the Word of God. We wish it might become true
so deeply that we decide it will be that way. We convince ourselves
and would convince others. There is no harm in such longing if we
subordinate it to God's will. He will perfect that which concerns us
and He who has begun a good work in us will finish it, so we leave
the details with Him. Rest assured that the Judge of all the earth will
do right and the reality will be more glorious than anything we can
now imagine.

JULY 17

GET OUT OF YOURSELF!

*He died for all, that they which live should not henceforth live unto
themselves, but unto him. . . .* 2 Corinthians 5:15.

TOO MANY CHRISTIANS live their Christian lives inside their heads;
it never gets out through hands and feet and lips. They need to get
out of themselves into witnessing and service and helping others—for
faith without works is dead. There are times, of course, when we
should withdraw into ourselves for self-examination and prayer.
Whether we are *extroverting* or *introverting,* we should live not for self
or others but "unto him," who was the perfect example.

GOD AND MAN

The man is become as one of us. . . .   Genesis 3:22.

"IN THE BEGINNING God. . . ." God made man and man was seduced by the tempter's words, "Ye shall be as gods." He entered a realm forbidden to him and all history is the sad consequence. Today man seeks to be God Himself and would usurp powers that belong only to the Almighty. He has painted himself into a corner and in desperation will turn one day to Antichrist, the man who would be God (2 Thessalonians 2:3,4). The answer to our dilemma is found in God who became man, the Word who became flesh and dwelt among us. He bore the penalty of man's transgression and began a new race of the sons of God. He redeems the soul, will raise the body, and redeem all creation from the curse. The issue is between God who became man and the man who would be God. Man himself, caught in the middle, must choose Christ or Antichrist, for our Lord said, "He that is not with me is against me . . ." (Matthew 12:30).

AND THEY KNEW HIM

I . . . will manifest myself to him.   John 14:21.

JESUS REVEALED HIMSELF to the Emmaus disciples as He walked with them, as He expounded the Scriptures, and as He broke bread in their home. He manifests Himself to us today in the same way, through the fellowship of the daily walk, through the Scriptures, and at home. He has promised to make Himself real to all who keep His commandments (John 14:21). Not in blinding vision, rare ecstasy, some weird and strange visitation, but along the road, through the Book, and at our table. This was not the Lord's Supper or a miraculous supper, but a common meal made uncommon by His hands. When they saw His hands, they must have seen the nail prints!

JULY 20

NOW

Now is the accepted time. . . .   2 Corinthians 6:2.

DO NOT LIVE in yesterday for it is past. Learn its lessons, then forget the things which are behind. Do not live in tomorrow for you cannot spend time you do not have. God is the Great I Am and so is His Son, the same yesterday and forever indeed but also the same *today.* We tend to dwell in the bygone and feed on its memories or keep going in the anticipation that tomorrow will be better. All you really have is this moment, this breath, this heartbeat. You cannot recall any hour that is past—how you wish you might! You cannot borrow a breath or a heartbeat from whatever supply the future holds. The only spending currency of time that you have is what you are spending while the seconds tick away as you read these words. All you have is NOW!

JULY 21

SOME KNOTS MUST BE CUT

Who is on the Lord's side? let him come unto me.   Exodus 32:26.

MOSES HAD TO act quickly when Israel worshiped the golden calf. It was no time to dicker with Aaron, hold conferences, quibble over the issue, take a vote. Some knots are not to be slowly unraveled, they must be cut promptly and on the spot. The situation will not wait. Drastic action alone will meet the emergency. Weak Aarons must not be tolerated. Somebody must stand in the door of the camp and rally the Levites. Unpleasant procedure is required. Today the world and most of the professing church dances before its golden calves. It is time for an angry Moses to grind idols into powder and mix it in the drinking water. Some knots must be cut. It takes too long to untie them.

JULY 22

ANSWERS

Ye are complete in him. . . .   Colossians 2:10.

A FRIEND SENT to me a bookmark that reads:

> Birds do not sing because they have an answer,
> They sing because they have a song!

The birds do not have all the answers, but they sing because they have a song within. We are told to consider the birds. They have their mishaps and miseries, but not even a sparrow falls without God's notice. The Christian does not have all the answers to the *whys* that baffle and perplex him, but he has the Answer in whom are gathered up all our problems. We see not yet all things put under Jesus, but we see Him and He is our song.

JULY 23

FROM GROANINGS TO GLORY

The whole creation groaneth. . . . We ourselves groan. . . . The Spirit itself maketh intercession for us with groanings. . . .
Romans 8:22,23,26.

ALL CREATION GROANS under the blight of sin awaiting the New Age. All the ecology excitement of these days finds here its explanation. We ourselves groan in our pain-racked bodies awaiting the resurrection. But we are not left to ourselves in this sad state. The Holy Spirit prays for us with unutterable groanings. If He groans for us, we might well agonize in prayer for ourselves! Unfulfilled, unrelieved, unutterable groaning up to now! The redeemed earth under the reign of our Lord will change us from groanings to glory!

JULY 24

A CHARGE TO KEEP

That good thing which was committed unto thee keep by the Holy
Ghost which dwelleth in us. 2 Timothy 1:14.

SOME HAVE FOUND fault with the old hymn that says:

> A charge to keep I have—A God to glorify,
> A never dying soul to save And fit it for the sky.
> CHARLES WESLEY

We do have a charge to keep and we need to hold fast to what we have so that no one steals our crown. Another old hymn asks, "Have we been true to the trust He left us?" It ought to humble us when we reflect on wasted time, lost opportunities, halfhearted service, good words we might have spoken, burdens we might have lightened. We are stewards who must give account. God will keep the deposit we left with Him, but He has also made a deposit with us. Are you a faithful keeper of the charge?

JULY 25

BRIDLE OR SPUR

Lord, I will follow thee. . . . Lord, suffer me first to go and bury
my father. Luke 9:57,59.

ONE PROSPECTIVE DISCIPLE in this passage was precipitate, over-hasty, impulsive, and needed to be restrained. Our Lord spoke later of the man building a tower and the king going to war, both of whom sat down first to count the costs and risks involved. Our Lord would have us deliberately consider the price of discipleship and not start out with a bang only to end in a bog. The second prospect was as slow as the other was fast and needed to be prodded with a stern, "Let the dead bury their dead: but go thou and preach the kingdom of God" (v.60). Do you need a bridle or a spur?

JULY 26

THE GUEST WHO WOULD GO ON

He made as though he would have gone further.   Luke 24:28.

OUR LORD IS a Gentleman. He will not force Himself upon us or come in where He is not wanted. He would have gone further, but He longed to manifest Himself to the Emmaus disciples. Have you not, in the company of someone you loved, moved as though you would be going, yet inwardly hoped you would be asked to remain? The deeper things of God pass on if we do not lay hold upon them. The Emmaus disciples earnestly constrained our Lord to abide with them for it was toward evening and the day was far spent. The *Guest who would go on* is also the *Guest who would come in.* He knocks at our door and if we open He will enter and the Guest will become the Host as He makes Himself known in the breaking of bread. Shame on us, Christian brothers, to keep Him standing there!

JULY 27

WHAT TO DO WITH YOURSELF

I am crucified with Christ. . . .   Galatians 2:20.

THE EMPHASIS TODAY is on self-improvement, self-realization, self-satisfaction. All sorts of courses and recipes and *secrets* abound on self-fulfillment. Even Christianity has become just a better way to have a good time. The Bible does not teach self-development but rather death to self. The Church is not an Old Adam Improvement Society. The only thing we should do with self is consent to its crucifixion and cooperate with God in the process. We do not crucify ourselves, it is the work of the Holy Spirit. We do not become robots. Paul said, "Nevertheless I live . . . yet not I. . . ." Christ lives in us and, as we allow Him to be Himself in us, there is less of us and more of Him. We are dead and our life is hid with Christ in God.

JULY 28

AT HOME

Absent from the body, and to be present with the Lord.   2 Corinthians 5:8.

TWO STRIKING WORDS are used here, one meaning to be away from home, the other to be among one's own people. The Christian is a pilgrim in a strange land. What joy it is to come home from weeks among strangers! The believer belongs to another country and what a prospect we have of going home! The true disciple can never make himself feel at home in this world. He is in a backslidden condition if he begins to integrate into the society of this age. My dear one's favorite song was "This World Is Not at Home." She is at home tonight and I am still making my way through these lowlands. I know what Paul means. I am anxious to become an absentee from this poor earth and shout "Present!" at my first roll call in heaven!

JULY 29

HOME BEFORE DARK

The night cometh, when no man can work.   John 9:4.

WHEN I WAS a boy growing up in the hills, it was a law of the Medes and Persians that I should be home before dark. That was understood and there were no exceptions. Night is settling on the world today and the time is short. We must work the works of God while it is day. We

Christians are not of the night nor of darkness. God is going to gather His children home before the final storm breaks. I want to get home before darkness settles on my little day. But the darkness precedes the dawn even as it follows the day. I want to get home where it is never dark for there is no night there.

JULY 30

REFINEMENT

Behold, I have refined thee, but not with silver; I have chosen thee in the furnace of affliction. Isaiah 48:10.

THE WORD *refinement* needs a Scriptural definition in the context of the Christian faith. When we say *refined,* we mean educated, cultured, with good taste and manners, elegant. All these should characterize a Christian, but one may have them all and not be a Christian. The refined Christian has been in the furnace of God's testing and has come out purged of dross and purified by the fire. His gold is refined, not mixed with an alloy. Such refinement is rare because it is very costly.

JULY 31

WHY DOESN'T GOD DO SOMETHING?

Wherefore dost thou forget us for ever and forsake us so long time? Lamentations 5:20.

SO SAID THE prophet and so say many today. Why does this sin and shame and sorrow and suffering have to be? Why did God let it start and why doesn't He stop it? If He is omniscient, He knows how it started, and, if He is omnipotent, He could end it. That is a foolish question like: "Can God make a rock so heavy He can't lift it?" He is not all-powerful, they say, if He can or if He can't. We can rack our brains until we wreck them on such puzzles. God *has* done something in Jesus Christ and all the questions are answered in Him, some already and some not yet but all eventually.

AUGUST 1

I BEING IN THE WAY

I being in the way, the Lord led me. . . . Genesis 24:27.

EVERYTHING DEPENDS ON our being in the way. God has not promised to lead and to bless us when we are in the wrong way. Sometimes the way seems long and hard and we may grow fearful that we have missed it. A traveler in the jungle said to his guide, "But there is no path, no road, no way." The guide replied, "There is no road, I am the way!" Our Lord is not the way-shower, He is *The Way.* When we abide in Him, we need no chart or compass. The Holy Spirit has come to guide us into all truth. He is the One called alongside to help. We may be perplexed at times and see not the way ahead but let us take our bearings and, if our hearts condemn us not, then let us take heart and keep going. We being in the way, He will lead us.

AUGUST 2

OUTNUMBERED

Fear not: for they that be with us are more than they that be with them. 2 Kings 6:16.

ELISHA'S SERVANT SAW only the visible host of the enemy. Elisha saw heavenly horses and chariots for the angel of the Lord encamped round about to deliver them that feared Him. When our Lord was arrested in the Garden, He seemed to be outnumbered by His adversaries, but He said to Peter, "Thinkest thou that I cannot now pray to my Father, and he shall presently give me more than twelve legions of angels?" (Matthew 26:53). That is a lot of angels! We are inclined to count ourselves as God's minority, but even statistics are on our side! There are more of us than there are of them!

AUGUST 3

WE'LL OVERTAKE THEM!

I shall go to him, but he shall not return to me.　2 Samuel 12:23.

THIS IS ONE of the few clear-cut affirmations in Scripture about reunion with our dear ones who have preceded us to heaven. It is taught, implied, intimated in many passages, but here is a concrete example where David rose from his weeping, dressed and resumed his normal habits, saying, "But now he is dead, wherefore should I fast? can I bring him back again?" We dwell so often on the gloomy fact that the dear one has gone not to return and forget that, if they and we are in the Lord, we shall soon overtake them! It is merely a matter of timing and it cannot be long at the longest. Things have not come to an end but to an interval. Wherefore should we fast?

AUGUST 4

EDUCATED IGNORANCE

But the natural man receiveth not the things of the Spirit of God: for they are foolishness unto him: neither can he know them, because they are spiritually discerned.　1 Corinthians 2:14.

THE NATURAL MAN can never be educated into apprehension of divine truth. In fact, the more wisdom of this world he accumulates, the more confirmed he is in error and the more moronic the Gospel appears. There is no hope in the supposition that a postgraduate course in secular knowledge will make it easier to see the things of the Spirit of God. It will only compound pride of intellect and harden resistance to the truth. Never forget that the wisdom of God is foolishness to men, which makes its believers fools in the eyes of men. Old Adam cannot be educated into a Christian.

AUGUST 5

THREE *D*S FOR ALL TIMOTHYS

Take heed . . . unto the doctrine. . . . 1 Timothy 4:16. *Endure hardness as a good soldier of Jesus Christ.* 2 Timothy 2:3. *Stir up the gift of God. . . .* 2 Timothy 1:6.

PAUL WOULD HAVE young Timothy well-grounded in what he believed. We have been entrusted with a sacred deposit, revealed truth, the Word of God. If a preacher is not doctrinally ready to preach, he is not ready. Then, he must be discipled, disciplined, trained in obedience. Only if we continue in the Word—the doctrine—are we disciples indeed. We must stir up the gift of God within us, that we may be burning and shining lights. But it is the dynamic of the Spirit, not human enthusiasm—old Adam worked up to a high pitch. *Stir* carries the idea of kindling the flame—*doctrine* that we may believe, *discipline* that we may behave, *dynamic* that we may burn! That is the true New Testament Timothy, believing, behaving, burning!

AUGUST 6

WELL IN HAND!

Neither shall any man pluck them out of my hand. . . . out of my Father's hand. John 10:28,29. *Behold, I have graven thee upon the palms of my hands. . . .* Isaiah 49:16. *My times are in thy hand. . . .* Psalms 31:15.

I CALL THIS "having the situation well in hand." Here is security for time and eternity. The palm of the hand is a well-protected place and that hand can fold into a fist if threatened! Not only ourselves but our times, all our circumstances, the day in which we live, the happenings of our lives—all these are under His control. Sometimes they are beyond our control, but "He's got the whole world in His hands." He not only leads us by His hand, He keeps us in His hand.

AUGUST 7

REASON AND REVELATION

All things continue as they were from the beginning of the creation. 2 Peter 3:4. *Oh that thou wouldest rend the heavens, that thou wouldest come down. . . .* Isaiah 64:1.

SCIENCE AND REASON see only the reign of natural law—cause and effect. The Spirit and revelation say that God breaks through and we pray that He may do it again. Science has devised engineering marvels that overwhelm the imagination, but look at what a mess we are in! Even the Church does not look for miracles and most of what goes on there can be accounted for by natural processes. The hungry-hearted child of God longs for a divine breakthrough, a mighty visitation that would strike rationalism dumb. Some go into extremism trying to work up supernatural experiences. The natural has its place, but we long for God to make bare His mighty arm not in the contranatural but the supernatural sense of His presence, the presence of Him who is greater than His laws and who is not imprisoned in the order He created.

AUGUST 8

IF THOU HADST BEEN HERE

If thou hadst been here, my brother had not died. John 11:32.

MARTHA AND MARY had sent a hurry call to Jesus, "He whom thou lovest is sick" (John 11:3). Instead of rushing to Bethany, our Lord abode two days where He was. Have you felt like complaining when

God did not come speedily to your help in time of need? "If Thou hadst been here, this wouldn't have happened." But if Jesus had hurried to Bethany, He would only have healed Lazarus. By waiting, He raised him from the dead! God's delay may bring a greater miracle than if He had answered our first prayer. Accept God's slow response. He is always on time—*His* time.

AUGUST 9

MIRACLES AFTER FORTY

For the man was above forty years old, on whom this miracle of healing was shewed.   Acts 4:22.

WHY DOES THE Holy Spirit give us this information about the lame man who was healed? Well, for one thing, when a miracle happens to anybody over forty, it is worth an extra verse! I am not so concerned about what the young generation is coming to as I am bothered about what has already come to the older generation! Youth is concerned today and young people will move in our meetings, but what is blocking revival so often is this stedfast and unmoveable crowd forty years old and over whose only response seems to be, "I move we accept this as information and be dismissed." Middle age is the bottleneck today and I can well understand the statement that everybody needs to be converted again after forty. There is a destruction that wasteth at noonday and the halfway mile is more perilous than the perils at sunrise or sunset. We need an outbreak of miracles after forty!

AUGUST 10

THE BROKEN NEST

As an eagle stirreth up her nest. . . .   Deuteronomy 32:11.

THE EAGLETS WOULD not learn to fly if the mother eagle did not tear up the nest. The early church at Jerusalem was thrown out of the nest by persecution to carry the Gospel in all directions. Some of us have known the tearing up of home, the loss of dear ones, that threw us out to fly or die. Then we learn that underneath are the everlasting arms. And how some smug, comfortable churches need their complacency wrecked, their comfortable indifference shattered that they may mount up with wings as eagles!

AUGUST 11

PRISONER OF THE LORD

The prisoner of Jesus Christ. . . . his prisoner. . . .   Ephesians 3:1;
Philemon 1:9;   2 Timothy 1:8.

PAUL WAS IN Nero's prison, but he was not Nero's prisoner. He was the prisoner of Jesus Christ. Back of all earthly incarceration, all dungeons of circumstance, all the jails of earth, stands our Lord and He is the Keeper of His people. Our times are in His hand. Stone walls do not a prison make nor iron bars a cage. However dark the shrouded room of sickness or sorrow, behind the dim unknown standeth God within the shadow keeping watch above His own. The Keeper of Israel does not slumber nor sleep. No man-made chains, no fetters of earth can bind our souls. We are prisoners of the Lord!

AUGUST 12

LIFE'S POOREST INVESTMENT

For what shall it profit a man, if he shall gain the whole world, and lose his own soul?   Mark 8:36.

HERE IS LIFE'S poorest investment, to gain even a whole world and lose one's soul. A coat of leopard skin hung in the window of a fur shop. A wag who walked by remarked, "That old cat was better off before he was worth so much!" A man who has gained riches at the expense of his soul may be the envy of some who pass by his mansion, but he has pauperized himself for all eternity. A man is just as rich as his investment in the bank of heaven. John wished that Gaius might prosper and be in health as his soul prospered. That is God's standard for a wise investor!

AUGUST 13

DOUBLE-MINDED

A double minded man is unstable in all his ways.   James 1:8.

JAMES TELLS US that the man who does not have God's wisdom is like a wave of the sea, unstable, ever-changing; such a man talks out of both sides of his mouth. He is like Erasmus who, when Luther was taking a firm stand come what may, could burnish *yes* until it sounded like *no* and *no* until it would pass for *yes.* Our yea should be yea and our nay, nay. When I see a dog coming toward me showing his teeth and wagging his tail, I never know which to believe. Let us make up our minds. We are never really *neither/nor* nor both. If we are not with our Lord, we are against Him and if we gather not with Him, we scatter abroad.

AUGUST 14

WHAT ARE YOU LOOKING AT?

While we look not at the things which are seen, but at the things which are not seen: for the things which are seen are temporal; but the things which are not seen are eternal.   2 Corinthians 4:18.

PAUL DESCRIBES HIMSELF as beset by trouble, perplexity, persecution, but not fainting because, though the outer man perish, the inner man is renewed daily while he looks not at the temporal but at the eternal. He looks toward the time when he shall exchange the tent of his body for an enduring home. He groans in his longing to be absent from the body and present with the Lord. That is not a tired old preacher morbidly longing to die. It is all a matter of what one is looking at, the seen or the unseen. Christians who have really caught a glimpse of glory bright are pilgrims and strangers anxious to get home.

AUGUST 15

HOW MUCH CAN HE PUT YOU DOWN FOR?

Lay up for yourselves treasures in heaven. . . . Matthew 6:20.

ONE FEELS LIKE stopping some song services where church members sing, "All to Jesus I surrender," "Take my life and let it be consecrated, Lord, to Thee," long enough to ask, "How much can the Lord put you down for? An hour at church, a few dollars in a church envelope?" The test of our affection is how much we will invest in the object of our love. The Macedonians first gave *themselves* unto the Lord. How much stock have you taken out in the bank of heaven, the cause of Christ? Dr. Webb-Peploe used to say, "On my travels I frequently buy gifts for my wife. Some of them may be poor choices, but she accepts them graciously because she knows that, before I gave her gifts, I first gave her my heart." Can God put you down for a total investment—self, service, substance?

AUGUST 16

BUT GOD. . . .

All these things are against me. Genesis 42:36. *Ye thought evil against me; but God meant it unto good. . . .* Genesis 50:20.

JOSEPH'S EARLY LIFE was filled with severest adversity. Sold into Egypt, thrust into prison, he might well have decided that all his early dreams were brainstorms. He might have asked, "What's the use?" But God turned the evil designs of men to the good of many. One cannot say, "All these things are against me," if he believes that all things work together for good to God's people. Throughout the centuries when things grew darkest there was daylight when God intervened. Stop counting all "these things" that seem against you. If you trust God, He is over all things, including "these things." Down the road, the way takes a turn and the sign reads BUT GOD!

AUGUST 17

THE MIRACLE LIFE

Christ liveth in me. . . .   Galatians 2:20.

THE CHRISTIAN LIFE is not merely a way of life, but Christ Himself living again in all who trust and obey Him. This life is miraculous in origin for it is the gift of God. It is miraculous in operation by the grace of God. It is miraculous in objective, the glory of God. There is so little of the miraculous in the Church today because most of her members are not living miracle lives. We have mostly an Old Adam Improvement Society of merely religious natural men who have never had the initial miracle of the second birth. We have developed a facsimile of the Christian experience without either the origin, operation, or objective of the original and the genuine. If we are what we have always been, we are not Christians. A Christian is a new creation.

AUGUST 18

BONE FIRE AND BONFIRE

His word was in mine heart as a burning fire shut up in my bones, and I was weary with forbearing, and I could not stay.   Jeremiah 20:9. *Many of them also which used curious arts brought their books together, and burned them. . . .*   Acts 19:19.

JEREMIAH WAS READY to give up prophesying and go into the motel business in a wilderness, but a holy compulsion inside him would not let him do it. A preacher had better not preach until preach he must. He may smother that flame and quench the Spirit, but he will have a holy heartburn. Rather let him make a bonfire of all his own loves and ambitions and all evil trash and treasure as did the Ephesians with their books of magic. If there is to be a holy bone fire there must be a bonfire!

AUGUST 19

STOCKS AND BONDS

He went away sorrowful: for he had great possessions. Matthew 19:22. *I would to God, that not only thou, but also all that hear me this day, were both almost, and altogether such as I am, except these bonds.* Acts 26:29.

THE RICH YOUNG Ruler's wealth kept him out of the Kingdom and many a man gains the world and loses his soul. Stocks and bonds can make it difficult to lay up treasure in heaven. Paul's stocks and bonds were of another sort, stocks for his feet and bonds for his wrists, but he could wish that kings had his heavenly treasure. The Scriptures do not teach the denial of money or its deification but its dedication. If we can be poor in spirit and rich at the bank well and good, but it is a rare combination. One may wear earthly chains and be a spiritual millionaire. Far better that than a capitalist in chains!

AUGUST 20

GET OUT OF THE "WOULDS"!

If thou wouldest seek unto God betimes, and make thy supplication to the Almighty. . . . Job 8:5.

"I WOULD IF I could." So said Moses and so said Jeremiah in a humility which God did not accept. God was saying, "You could if you would." Moses lamented that he was not eloquent, was slow of speech and of a slow tongue (Exodus 4:10). Jeremiah said, "I cannot speak: for I am a child" (Jeremiah 1:6). Humility is not thinking meanly of oneself, but rather it means not thinking of one's self at all. Get out of the "woulds"! We can do whatever God wants us to do as He works in us to will and to do of His good pleasure.

AUGUST 21

THE HOPE OF DYING

Willing rather to be absent from the body, and to be present with the Lord. 2 Corinthians 5:8.

PAUL HAD A desire to depart and be with Christ which is far better. A seasick man was leaning in agony over the rail when a friend said, "Cheer up! Seasickness never killed anybody." "Don't tell me that," groaned the suffering voyager, "it's the hope of dying that has kept me alive!" The Christian's hope of dying does help keep us alive through the trials and tribulations of this present time, for it speaks of heaven and seeing our Lord and reunion with dear ones gone before. The hope, not the dread, of dying can be a tonic, an elixir to the tired traveler in these lowlands. The best is yet to be and we can't lose for winning!

AUGUST 22

THE COURT OF PUBLIC OPINION

With me it is a very small thing that I should be judged of you, or of man's judgment. . . . 1 Corinthians 4:3.

PAUL SAYS OUR work is judged before three courts. The first is public opinion—what people think of us. But that is not the main test, for others do not know all the facts. Man's little *day* is not to be compared with the Great Day Coming. Men do not know "the whole truth and nothing but the truth" about us. What's done we partly may compute but know not what's resisted. We are not to make light of what others think or disregard helpful criticism, but the Court of Public Opinion is not the highest tribunal. Don't lose any sleep over what *they say*. It is a very small thing to be judged of men.

AUGUST 23

THE COURT OF PRIVATE JUDGMENT

I judge not mine own self. For I know nothing by myself; yet am I not hereby justified. . . .   1 Corinthians 4:3,4.

WE ARE NOT capable of judging our own selves and our work for we are too close to it and likely to color the verdict in our own favor. Even if our conscience is void of offense and our heart does not condemn us, we may not make correct appraisal. Things may not be right in the sight of God when they are satisfactory to us. We are too prejudiced in our own behalf to give an unbiased estimate. Many comfortable people, complacent in self-esteem, will get a great awakening one day when they face the Judge of all the earth.

AUGUST 24

THE COURT OF DIVINE JUSTICE

Therefore judge nothing before the time, until the Lord come, who both will bring to light the hidden things of darkness, and will make manifest the counsels of the hearts: and then shall every man have praise of God.   1 Corinthians 4:5.

EVERY MAN MUST give an account of himself to God and we must all appear before the Judgment Seat of Christ. Here we shall receive judgment tempered with mercy. The believer will be rewarded according to his works. Let us therefore not pass judgment on ourselves or on others until all the facts are in. The Judge of all men will do right and we must reserve our final appraisal for the final Court.

AUGUST 25

DEATH IS INCIDENTAL

This sickness is not unto death, but for the glory of God, that the Son of God might be glorified thereby. John 11:4.

LAZARUS'S SICKNESS WAS unto death in that he did die, but our Lord is saying that death was not the main objective. I am convinced that how Christians leave this world is not too important in God's sight. "Precious in the sight of the Lord is the death of his saints" (Psalms 116:15), but death is only the means to a greater end. Some Christians go out under unexplainable circumstances that do not seem to make sense. Consider the "others" in Hebrews 11:35–38. But God will raise all His children with new bodies and promote them to higher service. How they leave this world is not a major matter. The goal is the glory of God, not only in sickness but in everything, even death itself as our Lord told Peter (John 21:19).

AUGUST 26

ONLY GOD IS ANYTHING

So then neither is he that planteth any thing, neither he that watereth; but God that giveth the increase. 1 Corinthians 3:7.

GOD LAYS ASIDE His co-workers as the carpenter his tools. Some are castaways, disapproved. Some are old and spent. A preacher who once swayed multitudes fades out in seclusion. We have our day and some finish early, dying in full bloom. All that matters is that the work goes on, the building goes up. We are not mere pawns on a chessboard, for God is our Father, but we serve our generation by the will of God and then fall asleep and are laid with our fathers. The planters and builders come and go and are nothing—only God is anything and everything.

AUGUST 27

THE SUPREME COURT

For we must all appear before the judgment seat of Christ. . . .
2 Corinthians 5:10.

WE HAVE A date with Deity and an appointment with the Almighty. We cannot beg off or be excused. The Supreme Court is not nine old men in Washington but the Judgment Seat of Christ. We are not faultless to stand before that throne unless we are clad in His righteousness alone. In this day, when law and order seem on the way out and criminals get only a slap on the wrist, it is well to remember that the wages of sin remain the same and what men sow they still reap. The penalty has been paid and pardon provided if we accept the arrangement the Judge has made. Only then can we stand before the Throne in Him complete.

AUGUST 28

THE CREAM PITCHER

Ye make clean the outside of the cup and of the platter, but within. . . . Matthew 23:25.

RESTAURANTS SOMETIMES SERVE ordinary milk in a cream pitcher, but a cream pitcher does not change milk into cream. "It takes more than a better grade of china to heighten the flavor of indifferent tea." From pulpits today, a lot of skim milk is served in cream pitchers! The wrapper does not match the contents. The Bible abounds in figures of external appearance that belies what is within. "Whited sepulchres" (Matthew 23:27), ". . . in sheep's clothing, but inwardly they are ravening wolves" (Matthew 7:15). "They profess that they know God; but in works they deny him . . ." (Titus 1:16). ". . . for man looketh on the outward appearance, but the Lord looketh on the heart" (1 Samuel 16:7). We need to produce better contents instead of majoring on better cups!

AUGUST 29

ARE YOU HUNGRY?

I have esteemed the words of his mouth more than my necessary food. Job 23:12.

IT IS OFTEN said with regard to churchgoing: "Feed them and they will come." That is only partly true. Christians who love God's Word will come but not the unconverted. Hunger for God's Word is not a natural appetite. We are not born with it. It comes with the new birth when we begin with milk and should go on to meat. But the natural man has no appetite for heavenly food nor does he enjoy it. Trying to interest the unsaved man with deep spiritual truth is casting pearls before swine.

AUGUST 30

TRUTH BEFORE FREEDOM

If ye continue in my word, then are ye my disciples indeed; And ye shall know the truth, and the truth shall make you free. John 8:31,32.

WE HAVE NEVER heard more about freedom and had less of it than today. Our Lord declares that freedom is based on truth. "The truth shall make you free." But truth and freedom apart from Jesus Christ are abstractions. Verse 32 begins with "And," so we must go back to verse 31 to get the secret. "If ye continue in my word . . . ye shall know the truth." *Continue* means there must be a beginning and verse 31 was said to those who *believed* on Him. So we have faith that follows, continues in His Word, and produces freedom—freedom through faith that follows. Truth and freedom are not abstractions, they are found in a Person. "If the Son therefore shall make you free, ye shall be free indeed" (John 8:36).

AUGUST 31

GOD OF THE VALLEYS

Because the Syrians have said, The Lord is God of the hills, but he is not God of the valleys, therefore will I deliver all this great multitude into thine hand, and ye shall know that I am the Lord.
1 Kings 20:28.

WE ARE INCLINED to think of our God as the God of the hills, the lofty and exalted experiences of life. But He is also the God of the valleys, the dark and trying days, when the sun does not shine and the journey is long and painful. We shall surely be overcome by the enemy if we are *hill children* without the faith that will not shrink though pressed by many a foe in the lowlands of sorrow. Where there are mountains, there must be valleys. But there never was a winter that was not followed by spring. The Christian life is up and down, heights of fellowship with God and lofty vision but also the valleys, even of the shadow of death. But we need fear no evil for the God of the hills is with us when we travel the valleys below.

SEPTEMBER 1

SOMETHING TO REMEMBER

Lord, make me to know mine end, and the measure of my days, what it is; that I may know how frail I am. Psalms 39:4.

SOMEONE HAS SAID, "He remembereth that we are dust," and we had better remember it, too! This is not self-pity or self-depreciation. It is plain reality. We are creatures of the dust and our life is like a fleeting cloud, here today and gone tomorrow. This is not the false humility Moses and Jeremiah displayed when called to service or Elijah under the juniper. It is the honest recognition that, left to ourselves, we are nothing. Beside God we are zeros, but we also take meaning as do zeros beside numerals. He made us of dust, but He can make vessels to His honor when we are clay in the hands of the Potter.

SEPTEMBER 2

NEXT DOOR TO HEAVEN

There is but a step between me and death. 1 Samuel 20:3.

AND THERE IS but a step between me and heaven. As one grows old and the dearest of earth, the other half of one's life, goes on to the next world, things here lose their charm and we can hardly wait to see what lies beyond. To remain in the flesh is needful as long as God leaves us here, but we desire to depart and be with Christ which is far better —absent from the body—present with the Lord. A strange sense of being in two worlds at once possesses us. If we could break the barrier, we would have done it long before now! But until then we live next door to heaven.

SEPTEMBER 3

THE LOOKUP

And when these things begin to come to pass, then look up, and lift up your heads; for your redemption draweth nigh. Luke 21:28.

SOME OF LIFE'S valleys are so low that there is no lookout but there is always a lookup. We are walled around but not roofed over! The outlook today is cloudy, we are fogged in by foul conditions. There is no way out, but there is a way up. We need not drop our heads in despair or shake them in bewilderment. Our redemption draweth nigh. Sometimes God brings us to depths where the view all around is dark and desolate and we can escape only by taking off like a helicopter—straight up. Do not worry too much about your lookout but keep the lookup open!

SEPTEMBER 4

THE DRIFTERS

So then because thou art lukewarm, and neither cold nor hot, I will spue thee out of my mouth.   Revelation 3:16.

WE ARE FAMILIAR with the poem about the High Road and the Low. There is a third thoroughfare, the misty flats where the rest drift to and fro. They know neither height nor depth, they are neither cold nor hot. They are proud of their moderatism, which does not mean moderation; they know neither victory nor defeat. Life's greatest experiences do not come on the misty flats but on the heights, where we mount up as eagles, or the depths of adversity, where we walk and faint not, where stone walls do not a prison make nor iron bars a cage.

SEPTEMBER 5

LEAVE A WELL IN THE VALLEY!

Blessed is the man whose strength is in thee; in whose heart are the ways of them. Who passing through the valley of Baca make it a well. . . .   Psalms 84:5,6.

BACA IS THE Valley of Weeping. When we pass through it in sorrow and bereavement, let us leave behind a well of blessing from our sad experience so that others following after us may assuage their thirst, refresh their spirits, and cool their parched lips. Some of us drink today from such wells that others left in Baca. David himself has made millions his debtors through the centuries. Consider Bunyan in Bedford jail, Fanny Crosby in her blindness. And above all others, our Lord walked that Lonesome Valley and we have quenched our thirst at the well He left on that Via Dolorosa. Leave a well in Baca!

SEPTEMBER 6

ONE THING THOU LACKEST

One thing thou lackest: go thy way, sell whatsoever thou hast, and give to the poor, and thou shalt have treasure in heaven: and come, take up the cross, and follow me.   Mark 10:21.

LACKING ONE THING, the Rich Young Ruler lacked everything. He had great possessions, we are told, but he was a pauper for he had no investments in heaven. He had morals, manners, and money, but he never sold out to Jesus Christ. He would not become involved in that cause. We had better save our scorn until we have taken stock of ourselves. Multitudes of well-fixed church members have kept the law and have been interested in eternal life but have never made the Big Giveaway. The cause of Christ demands total involvement. We suffer the loss of all things, but all things are ours and having nothing we possess everything!

SEPTEMBER 7

ONE THING IS NEEDFUL

But one thing is needful: and Mary hath chosen that good part, which shall not be taken away from her.   Luke 10:42.

MARTHA WAS BUSY preparing a good meal and our Lord did not mean that it was unimportant. But Martha was flustered and bothered over matters of secondary importance and our Lord was emphasizing what matters most, our communion with Him. To hate father and mother in comparison to our love for Him was a similar emphasis. Even our religious activity, though sincere and well-intended, can take precedence over sitting at His feet. Ephesus was busy but had left her first love. (And we can be at so many church meetings that we neglect the home, which is the other side of the coin!)

SEPTEMBER 8

ONE THING I DO

This one thing I do, forgetting those things which are behind, and reaching forth unto those things which are before, I press toward the mark for the prize of the high calling of God in Christ Jesus.   Philippians 3:13,14.

I SHALL NEVER forget Dr. R. A. Torrey saying to me as a young preacher, "Young man, make up your mind on one thing and stick to it." The Christian life should be like a sword with one point, not like a broom ending in many straws. Such a single purpose forgets the past, reaches toward the future, and presses on. There is no time or place for side issues, diversions to the right or to the left. There is no place for hands on the plow with eyes looking back. Paul was a one-track man, but you can go a long way on one track!

SEPTEMBER 9

HE IS WITH US NOW

For I am in a strait betwixt two, having a desire to depart, and to be with Christ; which is far better. . . .   Philippians 1:23.

THE LAST FOR which the first was made—that was Paul's highest aspiration, to be with Christ. But do not forget that Christ is with us *now*. We are hampered by our limitations and not as aware of Him as we should be. There, no longer blinded by our eyes, we shall know as we are known and we shall be like Him for we shall see Him as He is. But He is with us all the days when we see through a glass as in a riddle and to know Him better now is our chief business. Tomorrow can wait and we have only today.

SEPTEMBER 10

DOTTED LINE

Not what I will, but what thou wilt. Mark 14:36.

WE DRAW UP our little programs and ask God to sign on the dotted line, to endorse, and to bless our plans. We arrange meetings and set up the order of service, then in a set prayer we ask God to set His approval on everything. Should we not rather ask God to set up the program, plan the proceedings, while we sign on the dotted line? True, we must plan ahead, but do we ask God for the plan? We wait until the structure is finished, then "dedicate" it, invoking the divine blessing. Did we begin it by asking God for the blueprints?

SEPTEMBER 11

FAITHFUL IN THE LEAST

Faithful in that which is least. . . . Luke 16:10.

IF WE HAVE been faithful in the little situation that seemed insignificant, we are in line for something better. It is easy to withold our best from what looks unworthy of all-out effort and save our best for the big day. But when is the big day? It may be that on that dull drear mission, when we seemed to be wasting our time, God did something more important than we ever dreamed. Count not that day lost when we did our best under most discouraging circumstances. The deed takes its value from the spirit in which we did it. He that is faithful over a few things shall be made ruler over many things.

SEPTEMBER 12

CLOAK AND PARCHMENTS

The cloke that I left at Troas with Carpus, when thou comest, bring with thee, and the books, but especially the parchments.
2 Timothy 4:13.

PAUL WAS REDUCED to a few bare necessities. As the Christian grows older and as we draw nearer to the end of our earthly days and to the end of the age, only a few things really matter and we are amazed at how much we can do without. After disaster has wrecked house and home, the survivors clutch a few things they managed to recover, which take on a new value. As when a dear one leaves us for heaven, little things become doubly precious because of tender memories. As when one looks through the other end of a telescope, the small becomes large and the large becomes small. Cloak and parchments, food and raiment, let us be content therewith!

SEPTEMBER 13

WHERE THERE'S HOPE THERE'S LIFE!

Which hope we have as an anchor of the soul, both sure and stedfast, and which entereth into that within the vail. . . .
Hebrews 6:19.

NOT ONLY IS it true that "where there's life there's hope," but where there's hope there's life. The New Testament is filled with hope and it centers in Jesus Christ within us, the hope of glory. Having this hope, we purify ourselves and, when trouble comes, we sorrow not as those who have no hope. It is hope in that which is to come that carries us through that which is now. Our redemption draws nigh and God will perfect that which concerns us. This hope makes us not ashamed. If you have grounds for hope, you have grounds for living!

SEPTEMBER 14

THE RESPONSIBILITY OF LISTENING

Take heed therefore how ye hear. . . .   Luke 8:18.

WHAT WE HEAR is important (Mark 4:24), but it is equally important *how* we hear. Receiving with meekness the engrafted Word (James 1:21) is a solemn duty. One reason why we do not have many great preachers is because we do not have many great listeners! It is just as important that Christians prepare to hear the sermon as it is that the preacher prepare to preach it. How few churchgoers ever think of readying ears and heart to hear the Word of God! We must be doers of the Word, of course, as well as hearers, but good hearing prepares for good doing.

SEPTEMBER 15

THE CHRISTIAN I MIGHT HAVE BEEN

O that thou hadst hearkened to my commandments! then had thy peace been as a river, and thy righteousness as the waves of the sea. . . .   Isaiah 48:18.

SADDEST OF ALL regrets will be this—the Christian I might have been. It will be the anguished moan of the lost who knew not the Lord. It will be the regret of countless Christians saved as by fire who might have been better saints if only they had made their experience of Christ their all-inclusive business. Many are backslidden and living in the world. And how many more, for lack of feeding on the Word, resting in the Lord, and exercising themselves unto godliness, never grow but are babes on milk instead of meat! The tragedy of the Might-Have-Beens!

SEPTEMBER 16

THROUGH TRIBULATION

We must through much tribulation enter into the kingdom of God. Acts 14:22.

THE SAINTS OF Lystra, Iconium, and Antioch were not promised an idyllic life to live happily after conversion but rather the same *pressure* our Lord promised His disciples (John 16:33) and Paul the new convert (Acts 9:16). In this day when all kinds of inducements are offered for joining the army, going to school, how to get rich without trying, how becoming an artist or an athlete can be a lot of fun, we need to find out early that to be a saint calls for faithful drudgery at times and is not just a better way to have a big time. Our Lord promised a cross and scars, not medals, down here. The honors are given out later. The Gospel is not entertainment and the way of the cross is not fun.

SEPTEMBER 17

THE STORM TEST

And the rain descended, and the floods came, and the winds blew, and beat upon that house. . . . Matthew 7:25,27.

IT IS THE storm that shows up the structure. The floods reveal the foundations. Counterfeit Christianity and fair-weather faith go down before the tempest. Paul puts it another way: "The day shall declare it . . . and the fire shall try every man's work of what sort it is" (1 Corinthians 3:13).

Whether foundation or superstructure, will it stand the test of rain and flood and fire?

SEPTEMBER 18

GLASS AND FIRE

A sea of glass mingled with fire. . . . Revelation 15:2.

SOME CHURCHES AND Christians are all glass in their cold dignity. Some are all fire in their religious excitement. The glass and the fire should mingle. We tend to swing from Rigor Mortis to St. Vitus. We freeze or we fry. Some appear to be en route to a funeral, some headed for a frolic. But we are invited to a *feast,* solid food with joyous fellowship.

SEPTEMBER 19

EXCHANGE

Beauty for ashes, the oil of joy for mourning, the garment of praise
for the spirit of heaviness. . . . Isaiah 61:3.

A POPULAR LITTLE song says:

> If tears were pennies
> And heartaches were gold,
> I'd have all the money
> My pockets would hold.

But God is able to transmute trouble into treasure, change the coinage of sorrow into the currency of joy. He gives songs in the night. We learn in the darkness what we never would have known in the day.

SEPTEMBER 20

STRANDED ON OMNIPOTENCE

Neither know we what to do: but our eyes are upon thee.
2 Chronicles 20:12.

JEHOSHAPHAT HAD REACHED that human extremity which is God's opportunity. Jeremiah (Lamentations 5) and Micah (7) were shut up to God in holy desperation. Throughout the Bible, those who received God's blessing were desperate. Consider Jacob at Jabbok, Moses at the Red Sea, Gideon and his three hundred, David and Goliath, the four lepers in the gate of Samaria, or Bartimaeus, the Syrophenician woman, Jairus. The Rich Young Ruler missed his blessing because he was not shipwrecked on God nor stranded on omnipotence!

SEPTEMBER 21

THE CARPENTER

Is not this the carpenter . . . ?   Mark 6:3.

WITH ONLY THIRTY-THREE years to spend on earth, my Lord spent thirty of them, the hidden years at Nazareth, preparing for three years of public ministry; He did not visit world capitals in a spectacular career. How different would His life have been if it had been planned by a manager and a public relations expert! For the first thirty years, the Carpenter glorified the ordinary. The Christian life is not a hectic round of sensational mountaintop experiences. It is living by the Spirit in the will of God day by day in home and shop, plying the daily task with busier feet because the secret soul a holier strain repeats.

SEPTEMBER 22

WE KNOW IN PART

We see through a glass, darkly. . . . 1 Corinthians 13:12.

IN THIS SIN-WRECKED world, strange things happen that do not make sense. Christians are not immune to or exempt from accidents, disease, heartache, disappointment, and tragedy. There are no easy answers and much we simply cannot understand. We have to table many a matter for future reference. I have several such items on my list! They are not complaints but conundrums, puzzles to be pieced together later in another world.

SEPTEMBER 23

WHERE ELSE CAN WE GO?

Lord, to whom shall we go? John 6:68.

PETER GIVES THREE reasons for being a Christian. He begins with the poorest, but it will do to start. It is a matter of alternatives. If we do not take Jesus' way, what else can we do? What are the other options? Look up any other road and what do you see? It comes to this: it is Jesus Christ or else. There is only one Book that has the Answer and Jesus Christ is that Answer. I do not understand everything in the Book, but I stand on everything in it. I look every other direction and I see only depravity, despair, and death. Where could I go but to my Lord?

SEPTEMBER 24

WONDERFUL WORDS OF LIFE

Thou hast the words of eternal life.   John 6:68.

PETER ADVANCES TO a second and better stage in his confession. Our Lord had already said, "Except ye eat the flesh of the Son of man, and drink his blood, ye have no life in you" (John 6:53). When many of His disciples stumbled at this pronouncement, He explained it: "The words that I speak unto you, they are spirit, and they are life" (John 6:63). We feed on the living Word as we feed upon the written Word. There is something about His words that is different from all other words. They are living and when planted they sprout and grow. Peter did not understand all of them, did not always live up to what they required, but he never doubted their origin, their quality, and power. Hear them, hide them in the heart, heed them by being a doer of them, and we are made aware of a *new life*.

SEPTEMBER 25

WE BELIEVE AND KNOW

And we believe and are sure that thou art that Christ, the Son of the living God.   John 6:69.

TO BELIEVE IS one thing; to know is another. Some believe in Christ, but they do not have certainty. It is possible to accept certain facts about our Lord and yet not have personal knowledge of Him. I believed that my dear wife loved me and was true to me, but, more than that, I *knew it*. Should we be less persuaded concerning our Lord? Paul knew *whom* he had believed. Christianity today is tragically weak here. It lacks the unshaken certainty that is sure He is the Son of the living God.

SEPTEMBER 26

FAR BETTER

*For I am in a strait between two, having a desire to depart, and
to be with Christ; which is far better. . . .*   Philippians 1:23.

WHAT IS IT like over there, where our departed loved ones have gone?
If they are Christians, one thing we know: with them it is *far better,*
better than it ever was here or could be. We would not wish them back
in this wreck of a world, though our eyes are blinded with tears at
their passing. When they left us, they took no turn for the worse. How
could they when "all things work together for good"? How could they
when they departed to go where it is *far better?*

SEPTEMBER 27

THINK IT OVER

*For which of you, intending to build a tower, sitteth not down
first . . . ? Or what king, going to make war against another king,
sitteth not down first. . . .*   Luke 14:28,31.

THE MAN BUILDING a tower and the king going to war *sat down first*
and deliberated on the cost and conduct of their venture. A quick,
snap-judgment decision is always dangerous, whether in marriage,
business, or the salvation of the soul. Faith in Christ involves discipleship and, while salvation is free, it means utter surrender of all we are
and have. This is the other side of the coin. Jesus paid it *all, all* to
Him I owe. God wants us to understand what we are doing and to
mean business. Think it over!

SEPTEMBER 28

BURDENS

Cast thy burden upon the Lord. . . . Psalms 55:22. *Bear ye one another's burdens. . . . For every man shall bear his own burden.* Galatians 6:2,5.

ALL OUR FEARS and doubts, all our heartaches and problems, all our unanswered *why*s can be left with God and what a relief! But we cannot pass the buck of personal responsibility to be the stewards of what He has entrusted to us. We must share the burdens of our fellow Christians and help them bear their load. We cannot wash our hands of our own duty, but we, as the burden, belong to Him and so does the wisdom to bear and to share. This mutual exchange of burden-bearing is part of the glorious life of the Christian family. There is His burden, our burden, and my burden.

SEPTEMBER 29

NOT AS THE WORLD GIVETH

Peace I leave with you, my peace I give unto you: not as the world giveth, give I unto you. John 14:27.

"THERE IS NO peace . . . to the wicked." The world offers false peace to dull the senses, deaden the conscience, quieten the nerves, but it cannot give peace. I remember the dear woman who stood in a little meeting long ago to thank God for "a deep, settled peace which the world didn't give and can't take away." We never heard so much about peace and security as now and never had less of it. Only peace with God through faith in His Son and the peace of God which garrisons our hearts and minds as we make our requests known with thanksgiving—only these can rest the soul. It is peace *not as the world giveth.*

SEPTEMBER 30

WHY DO THE WICKED REJOICE?

Wherefore doth the way of the wicked prosper? Wherefore are all they happy that deal very treacherously? Jeremiah 12:1.

JEREMIAH WAS NOT the only one who has wondered why the wicked often appear happier than the righteous, why worldlings sometimes seem to have a better time than the saints. The reason is not hard to find. The worldling enjoys the excitements of the flesh, the creature comforts of the natural man, and the excesses of sin. His laughter is as the crackling of thorns under a pot (Ecclesiastes 7:6). The Christian is often sore beset by the powers of darkness and is conscious of his sins and shortcomings. His goal is not happiness but holiness and in the world he has been promised tribulation, pressure. He is in training for service above and is not on a picnic but a pilgrimage in the steps of One who was a Man of sorrows and acquainted with grief.

OCTOBER 1

ALL SUNSHINE MAKES THE DESERT

It is good for me that I have been afflicted; that I might learn thy statutes. Psalms 119:71.

I LOVE SUNNY days and longingly sing about the land of unclouded skies. But if we had no clouds and rain, we would starve to death. Even thunder and lightning are necessary to clear the atmosphere. In the world to come, we shall not know storm and tempest, but this earth is so geared that we cannot do without it. "Into each life some rain must fall, Some days must be dark and dreary." If we have no chastening, we are bastards and not sons. So praise God for the dark days when often our sweetest lessons are learned as also songs in the night. All sunshine would mean a desert!

OCTOBER 2

IN THE PRESENCE OF ANGELS

There is joy in the presence of the angels of God over one sinner that repenteth. Luke 15:10.

THIS JOY IS said not to be among the angels (although that is true also, I am sure), but in their presence. They share it undoubtedly, but who else is there to do the rejoicing? The saints, of course! It must include loved ones in glory thrilled maybe at the conversion of a dear one on earth. It must include faithful preachers and others seeing the answer to their prayers and witnessing while on earth. This tells us more than the fact of their rejoicing, it shows that they are conscious and aware of things happening down here. It reveals the presence of angels who never walked down here, but in whose company we celebrate over there.

OCTOBER 3

ALMOST HOME

The time of my departure is at hand. 2 Timothy 4:6.

HOW GOOD TO be almost home! How pleasant it was in the old days when the train neared journey's end, my dear one, and our little dwelling place! Today the home over there beckons and the dear one waits again. God grant us to end well! I am not at home here. I have a few rooms and a few books and a bed, but I'm not home yet. God help me to sit loose to earth and prime my soul for heaven! There is nothing morbid in longing to be absent from the body and present with the Lord. That is heavenly homesickness. It is perfectly natural for a Christian who belongs over there anyway. He's almost home!

OCTOBER 4

MAN AND GOD

Ye shall be as gods. . . . Genesis 3:5. *The Word was made flesh. . . .* John 1:14. *He as God sitteth in the temple of God. . . .* 2 Thessalonians 2:4.

HISTORY IS THE long story of man trying to be God. He has been at it ever since Satan brought about his fall in Eden. He has done wonders, but, amidst all his scientific marvels and technological triumphs, his heart is empty and the whole world groans in travail. The peace and security he longs for, the new world he tries to create come only by Jesus Christ—God who became Man. Man without Christ will end one day under the man who would be God—Antichrist. Those who trust Christ await His return and His Kingdom. The issue is: God who became Man and the man who would be God.

OCTOBER 5

OBEDIENCE, THE PROOF OF RELATIONSHIP

For whosoever shall do the will of my Father which is in heaven, the same is my brother, and sister, and mother. Matthew 12:50.

I HEARD RECENTLY of a piece of land offered as a gift to a church but with certain stipulations as to the use of it. Salvation is the free gift of God with no strings attached, but the believer becomes a disciple and obedience is the evidence of his sonship. Trusting Jesus as Saviour involves confessing Him as Lord. We have filled churches with cheap believers who seem never to have learned that salvation is free but costs us all we are and have in discipleship. The Great Commission bids us make disciples, not merely believers.

OCTOBER 6

COMFORTED TO COMFORT

Who comforteth us in all our tribulation, that we may be able to comfort them which are in any trouble, by the comfort wherewith we ourselves are comforted of God. 2 Corinthians 1:4.

SUCH IS THE ministry of "the God of all comfort." We are not comforted just to be comforted, but that we may comfort others. We are not ends but means to an end. When we store God's blessings and do not pass them on, we stagnate and become selfish. We are saved to serve. The favors of God turn sour when hoarded for ourselves. The Christian who spends his time reading devotional books for his own enjoyment finds that the sweetness turns bitter if he does not become a channel of blessing. We are not saltcellars but saltshakers to scatter our blessings everywhere we go.

OCTOBER 7

DON'T MAKE IT TOO HARD

For my yoke is easy, and my burden is light. Matthew 11:30.

WE SOMETIMES MAKE the Christian life much harder than it is. If it were as difficult to enter into and to walk in as some imagine, most poor souls would give up in despair. To be sure there are heights and depths beyond our comprehension. If we could understand it, there wouldn't be much to it! I do not understand electricity, but I am not going to sit around in the dark until I do! The keys to the Kingdom are conversion and childlikeness (Matthew 18:3). His Commandments are not grievous. If we delight ourselves in the Lord, He will give us the desires of our hearts. The laboring and the laden are invited to His rest. He offers peace and joy to those who trust and obey. Hair shirts and self-inflicted austerities are not on His program. The ways of wisdom are pleasant ways and all the paths are peace.

OCTOBER 8

DON'T MAKE IT TOO EASY

If any man will come after me, let him deny himself, and take up his cross, and follow me. Matthew 16:24.

SOME MAKE THE Christian life too easy. To them, casting their care on the Lord means dismissing and disregarding serious responsibilities under the pretense of trust. Our Lord made discipleship hard and lost many prospective followers because He called them to a pilgrimage—not a parade, to a fight—not to a frolic. We are to endure hardness, overcome the world, and not merely endure it. We must strive to enter in at the strait gate, and work out our salvation with fear and trembling. Few there be who travel the narrow way and those who do will often be the objects of scorn. There is Scripture on both sides, making it too hard and making it too easy. A proper view of both will make for balanced living. The Saviour gives us the perfect example. A Man of sorrows and acquainted with grief, He offered joy and peace.

OCTOBER 9

LOOKING AND LIVING

Teaching us that . . . we should live soberly, righteously, and godly, in this present world; Looking for that blessed hope. . . .
Titus 2: 12,13.

TWO RELIGIOUS LEADERS of prominence have stated in their own ways that they have not been too excited about the Lord's return—preferring the experience of a living Christ present in their lives now to a coming Christ returning sometime in the future. They make it seem almost as though one has to choose between the two, a present reality or a future hope. Why not have both? In his words to Titus, Paul certainly stresses both living and looking. We do not have to pick one of two alternatives. The New Testament always ties up prophetic doctrine with practical duty. Having the hope of His coming, we purify ourselves now!

OCTOBER 10

BE THYSELF IN ME

Christ liveth in me. . . .   Galatians 2:20.

THE CHRIST-INDWELT BELIEVER may well pray, "Lord Jesus, be Thyself in me, release Thy powers in my life as much as possible." He has no limitations, but we have. Our bodies and minds are restricted and we see through a glass as in a riddle. We want His fullness to the full extent of our capacity. Later, when we have new faculties in another world, we can know and enjoy His presence and power without limit, but we earthbound creatures understand only in part. How much and how fully Christ can be Himself in us at present is an interesting subject. Certain it is that we could know Him better now than we do. How much divine power is possible for these minds and bodies is not measurable except to say as much as we need for our good and His glory. But we are generally far short of the possibilities and subsist on crackers and cheese with tickets to the banquets of His grace. Pray that He may be to you all He can under present conditions!

OCTOBER 11

A TIME FOR ANGER

And when he had looked round about on them with anger. . . .
Mark 3:5.

IT IS TIME we rediscovered how much the Bible has to say about the wrath of God. It is time we remembered our Lord's look of anger, His driving the traders out of the temple, His denunciation of the scribes and Pharisees. It is time we called to mind that He will return in vengeance on His adversaries (2 Thessalonians 1:7–9). It is the other side of love and, if there is a place for it in God's heart, there is room for it in the hearts of His people if for the same reason and expressed in the same way. We need an outbreak of holy indignation!

OCTOBER 12

UNTIL OUR TIME IS UP

Nevertheless to abide in the flesh is more needful for you.
Philippians 1:24.

PAUL WAS HOMESICK for heaven, desiring to depart and be with Christ which is far better. But his time on earth was not up. When old age comes or dear ones leave us for heaven, we long to go, too, so we pine away among our memories or count the days until our deliverance. But:

> Something remains for us to do or dare,
> Even the oldest trees some fruit may bear.

God has left us here for some purpose and we do well to find out what we may do in the time that is left. We have all eternity ahead but only a few days to finish our work here. It is needful that we abide in the flesh a little longer. Let us make this as good as possible before we reach the *far better!*

OCTOBER 13

WE'LL SOON FIND OUT!

Then shall I know even as also I am known.   1 Corinthians 13:12.

ONE OF THESE days Jesus is coming or I am going and then I shall find out what the next world is really like. Think of it, we are living every moment with the greatest of all mysteries ready to explode! How can we take it so casually, how can we be so blasé, on the verge of eternity all the time? I marvel that I ever get used to that and live as though I were going to stay here forever. Every day, every hour ought to be exciting, loaded with expectancy since anything can happen anytime. A whole eternity of wonder is always just a step, just a heartbeat away. "Lord, teach me to number my days!"

OCTOBER 14

SHARPENING THE AXE

If the iron be blunt, and he do not whet the edge, then must he put to more strength. . . . Ecclesiastes 10:10.

A DULL AXE means harder work and we lose no time when we sharpen the edge. The Christian in particular and the Church in general both need to stop chopping wood long enough to whet the blade. Hours out for the Word and prayer and a week out from regular church work to revive the saints is a wise investment. We save time that might be spent in a hospital later if we had a checkup now. It is poor business to add more wheels to the machinery and increase the work load when the power is low. When we are too busy to *sharpen the axe,* we are too busy!

OCTOBER 15

THE JUDGE WILL DO RIGHT

Shall not the Judge of all the earth do right? Genesis 18:25.

WE ARE INCLINED to wonder sometimes how it will be in the world to come. In our wishful thinking, we imagine blissful reunion with dear ones we have loved and lost for a while. But then there sometimes comes the chilling thought that maybe God will not do it that way.

After all He has not told us very much about our future relations with our loved ones. But we need not worry. The Judge of all the earth will do right. And that does not mean in a cold judicial sense, for the Judge is also our Father and what He does will be mixed with love and joy. We may be certain it will be lovingly and joyfully right, not just right. He knows now our frame and remembers that we are dust and He will know what is happily best when we are no longer dust but His resurrected children.

OCTOBER 16

FOR THE BIRDS

Behold the fowls of the air. . . .   Matthew 6:26.

THIS MORNING THE wood thrush, putting on an early concert in my backyard, reminded me of how much I owe to my feathered friends who have sung for me through the years free of charge. Since those precious boyhood days in the country long ago, I have been indebted to the birds who have brightened many a day through generation after generation of cardinals, meadowlarks, mockingbirds, vireos, and warblers and many, many more. They have had their troubles, too, and adversity has haunted them as well as me, but they keep singing, not because they have found an answer, but because they have a song. They still sing the same tunes, thank the Lord, and this mad age has added no new beats. God has brought them through and not a sparrow falls without our Father.

OCTOBER 17

IT WON'T LAST FOREVER BUT WE WILL!

Now for a season . . . ye are in heaviness. . . .   1 Peter 1:6. *After that ye have suffered a while. . . .*   1 Peter 5:10. *For our light affliction, which is but for a moment. . . .*   2 Corinthians 4:17.

WE ALL KNOW that there is a sense in which time is relative. Thirty minutes in a dentist's chair may seem longer than a whole week's vacation. Suffering may seem endless, but it won't last forever and our trials are "for a season," "a while," "for a moment." It will help if we think in terms of what is everlasting, for we are to be somewhere forever and a hundred years is but a nick of time in the sight of Him with whom a thousand years are as but a day and a day as a thousand years. In that very statement concerning the Almighty, you have the two aspects of time as relative. A thousand years can condense into a day or stretch into a millennium. Whether millennia or moments, we are not here to stay, but we are to stay—somewhere! Don't magnify the interval until it blocks out the eternal!

OCTOBER 18

TRUTH IN LOVE

But speaking the truth in love. . . .   Ephesians 4:15.

SOME SPEAK THE truth without love. Some preach love but have not the truth. So we swing from severity to sentimentality, from vinegar to sugar. It is one of Satan's cleverest tricks: major on one good aspect to the extent that we lose the balance of another good point that would maintain the equilibrium. Tenderness can be overdone to the loss of sternness, the sweetness can become *sticky.* Jeremiah mixed the elements and above all so did our Lord. Consider Him!

OCTOBER 19

CURE FOR SELF-PITY

Like as a father pitieth his children, so the Lord pitieth them that fear him. For he knoweth our frame; he remembereth that we are dust.   Psalms 103:13,14.

SELF-PITY CAN BECOME a ruinous habit. We weaken our powers feeling sorry for ourselves and defeat ourselves in advance before the battle begins. We do not know all the facts anyway and may be lamenting something that may be God's providence working things out for our good, as they always do to them that love God and are the called according to His purpose. He knows our frame and He expects from us only what His grace will enable us to do. Do not count on yourself and then you will not be disappointed. Count on God and again you will not be disappointed! Our Father pities His children. Let Him do it—don't pity yourself!

OCTOBER 20

I'M NOT AN ORPHAN

I will not leave you comfortless [*orphans*]   . . . . John 14:18.

I HAVE BEEN left a widower, lonely indeed. I am a pilgrim and a stranger on the earth, but I am not an orphan. As the song puts it, "I'm glad I'm a member of the family of God." God is my Father. Jesus is my Brother. The dear ones in glory have preceded me and I shall soon overtake them. My Lord is coming and all the saints here and over there will be reunited. We shall sit down with Abraham and Isaac and Jacob in the Kingdom of God. It is logical to believe that we shall also sit with all the saints. What a family and I am not left an orphan! He will come for me as He has said.

OCTOBER 21

TRIP TO THIRD HEAVEN

A man . . . caught up into paradise, and heard unspeakable words, which it is not lawful for a man to utter. 2 Corinthians 12:3,4.

GOD HAS NOT told us more about the world to come because, with our present faculties, we could neither receive nor reveal it, take it in or give it out—as a child might try to understand nuclear physics. Paul visited Paradise, but could not tell us what he heard. Our present equipment of body and mind is not geared to apprehend what God has prepared for us. It is revealed by the Spirit and in the Word as far as it has pleased God to make it known. He has told us enough to whet our appetites. The crumbs make us want the cake!

OCTOBER 22

A MATTER OF COMMON SENSE

Yea, and why even of yourselves judge ye not what is right? Luke 12:57.

THE BIBLE DOES not tell us much about recognition of our loved ones in heaven. May it not be that He expects us as a matter of common sense to accept that as a foregone conclusion? Such an inference requires no special illumination. Surely we shall not know less than we do now! It is implicit and inherent in the nature of God's purpose to perform what He has begun. What is holiest here below must forever live and grow. Common sense tells me that God will not dash to the ground the precious treasures of the heart we gathered here.

OCTOBER 23

UNDERSTANDING THE TIMES

*And of the children of Issachar, which were men that had under-
standing of the times, to know what Israel ought to do. . . .*
1 Chronicles 12:32.

THESE MEN HAD more than a knowledge of the times. News commen-
tators today have great knowledge of the times, but they do not
understand them in the light of God's Word. These children of Issachar had the kind of understanding that produced knowledge, the
practical knowledge of what God's people ought to do. This world
does not understand the times nor does it know what to do nor would
it do it, if it did understand. God's people ought to know what to do
because they do understand the times and, knowing the season, that
it is high time to wake up!

OCTOBER 24

MISSIONARY AT HOME

As my Father hath sent me, even so send I you.   John 20:21.

"WHOM SHALL I send, and who will go for us?" (Isaiah 6:8). "As thou
hast sent me into the world, even so have I also sent them into the
world" (John 17:18). The missionary picture abroad has changed and
so has the preaching ministry at home. We no longer go with pith
helmet to clear the jungles and kill lions and "convert the heathen"
as they used to say. Church work here has become a new ball game,
as we say now. What is the modern challenge, the corresponding call
to courage and sacrifice now? We have another kind of jungle and
other kinds of savages, but the challenge is just as great. To be a
Christian today calls for everything, the grain of wheat dying to live.
"So send I you" . . . today!

OCTOBER 25

CLIMATE AND CONSCIENCE

And herein do I exercise myself, to have always a conscience void of offence toward God, and toward men.   Acts 24:16.

THEY TELL US that times have changed, that we live in a new moral climate and must learn to live with it. I also have a conscience and must live with it. Paul lived in an evil day and the spiritual climate was bad. He wrestled with principalities and powers of the world of darkness. He was most concerned to have a good conscience. He is a foolish man who comes to terms with this world at the expense of his soul. We have to live with ourselves and, while everybody is majoring on how to get along with the times, let us remember that we are not thermometers to register the prevailing temperature but thermostats to change it.

OCTOBER 26

POINT OF NO RETURN

He shall not return to me.   2 Samuel 12:23.

SO SPOKE DAVID concerning his dead son. There is no record that those who were raised from the dead, like Lazarus, reported on their experiences after death. The spirit, absent from the body and present with the Lord, does not return to fill us in on the next world. The dragonfly is not returning to us as grubs in the slime. The butterfly does not communicate with the chrysalis. It is well that the departed dear ones do not visit us. Soon we shall break the barrier and all will be made plain. The cocoon will open in due time!

OCTOBER 27

YOU AND YOUR BURDEN

Cast thy burden upon the Lord, and he shall sustain thee. . . .
Psalms 55:22.

IT IS AN old illustration, but it came to mind recently with full force. A pedestrian carrying a heavy load was picked up by a motorist. He sat down in the automobile but kept his burden on his shoulder. The motorist asked why he didn't put it down. "Well," he replied, "you are so kind to carry me, I didn't want to bother you with this extra weight." So do we Christians sometimes trust the Lord to save our souls but insist that we must carry our burdens. He can sustain both you *and* your burden, your mind, your way, your times, your troubles. Put it all down. Cast all your care on Him. He careth for you. Why not let Him do it?

OCTOBER 28

WHAT PEACE WE OFTEN FORFEIT!

*It is vain for you to rise up early, to sit up late, to eat the bread
of sorrows: for so he giveth his beloved sleep.* Psalms 127:2.

"O WHAT NEEDLESS pain we bear, all because we do not carry everything to God in prayer." The Psalmist reproves us for rising up early and sitting up late with our worries when God, the Night Watchman of the Universe, is on duty and never sleeps. Could we but believe that He ever keeps watch above His own, that nothing escapes His notice, that all things work together for our good, we would not be the insomniacs and nervous wrecks that we are, living from pill to pill, sedative to sedative, trying to conquer needless pain and find departed peace. Some pains are necessary and some grief profitable, but, for much of both, there is balm in Gilead and we have not because we ask not.

OCTOBER 29

FEED YOUR FAITH AND STARVE YOUR DOUBT!

Lord, I believe; help thou mine unbelief.   Mark 9:24.

THIS FATHER OF a demonized boy had both faith and unbelief, but he took sides with his faith against his unbelief. Whatever we feed grows stronger. What we starve dies eventually. Your faith may be small, even as a grain of mustard seed, but feed it on the Word and exercise it unto godliness and it will gain strength by the day. Pay no attention to your doubts, no matter how feelings may clamor, and they will grow weaker. It is as simple as that. I did not say as easy as that, for Christian maturity is not reached easily, but it is as plain as that if we but follow it.

OCTOBER 30

REFUGEES

We . . . who have fled for refuge. . . .   Hebrews 6:18.

NEVER HAS HISTORY seen so many refugees as in this sad century. All over this unhappy world uncounted multitudes have had to leave home and country for safety elsewhere. Our hearts are wrung by the spectacle of frightened parents and hungry children tramping highways, loaded on overcrowded trains and boats and planes bound for new homelands. But the refugees of earth are not all victims of war. Everywhere people not touched by war and living in their own homes are nevertheless looking for a hiding place from the storm and stress of today. The Bible speaks often of refuge, our God, our Rock of Ages, a high place, a shelter in time of storm, and our Saviour bids the weary and heavy laden come to Him for rest. We are all refugees in this wrecked and ruined world. Have you found in God your hiding place?

OCTOBER 31

CARRY YOUR UMBRELLA!

And all things, whatsoever ye shall ask in prayer, believing, ye shall receive. Matthew 21:22.

WHEN IT COMES to praying in faith, most of us pray for rain but do not carry our umbrellas. We do not expect the answer according to Mark 11:24. One great Bible teacher was for a while perplexed by the grammar of that verse, "Believe that ye receive them, and ye shall have them." But finally he stopped worrying about the grammar and believed God! The mountain moves when we ask in faith (Matthew 21:21). "But let him ask in faith, nothing wavering" (James 1:6). "According to your faith be it unto you" (Matthew 9:29).

Carry your umbrella!

NOVEMBER 1

STUB OF A SWORD

Strengthen me . . . only this once. . . . Judges 16:28.

SAY WHAT YOU will about Samson—and grievous were his failures —a merciful God granted his last request and let power not his own flow through him. Sometimes when the war is almost over, when our strength is spent, and our opportunities have passed, God grants to His servants a final triumph and we go down in one last victory though we fight that battle with broken weapons.

> Strong is the foe who advances,
> Snapped is my blade, O Lord,
> See their proud banners and lances
> But spare me the stub of a sword.

NOVEMBER 2

NO QUESTIONS ASKED

I will see you again. . . . And in that day ye shall ask me nothing.
John 16:22,23.

OUR LORD DID not say, "When I see you again, I will answer all your questions." He said, "You won't ask any questions!" Our minds and hearts are filled with *why*s and we can hardly wait to hear the answers. But when we see Him we will not bother to bring up those questions. They will vanish in the glory of His presence. He will not answer them for we will not ask them! We see not yet all things put under Him. There is much that puzzles us for we see through a glass as in a riddle. We do not know all the answers, but He *is* the Answer. Our *why*s will no longer have significance. Don't hang on to them now for they will be as a mist before the rising sun. Everything will clear up one day. No questions asked. The Answer will have come!

NOVEMBER 3

FALLING APART

Thy word have I hid in mine heart, that I might not sin against thee. Psalms 119:11.

SOMEBODY PASSED ON to me recently a precious nugget: "If you see a Bible that is falling apart, it probably belongs to someone who isn't!" A well-worn Bible speaks volumes. Through the centuries, the old Book has kept unnumbered millions from coming unstuck, cracking up, and going to pieces. It has saved marriages from collapse, families from destruction, and many a battered soul has made it through a stormy life with the help of a ragged Bible thumbed with reverence and sobbed over in the small night hours when everything seemed lost. It has healed more hearts than all the counselors and prevented more breakdowns than all the psychiatrists. Reading it until it falls apart will hold us together!

NOVEMBER 4

RIGHT QUICK

The king's business required haste.   1 Samuel 21:8.

WHEN I WAS a boy, my father had a habit of calling me to do things with the summons, "Come, right quick!" I didn't mind the *come* but the *right quick* irritated me sometimes. He didn't mean, "Take your time, think it over, come if you feel like it." I had the impression that I had better feel like it! Father considered himself to be the head of the house and the rest of us were inclined to agree with him. I didn't talk back. We didn't have much dialogue in those days! The big word with God is *now*. If we are going to get anything done for Him, we had better get at it *now*. He is the *I Am*, the Eternal Contemporary. And the time is short. He would have us come and go and do *right quick!*

NOVEMBER 5

DEMAS

For Demas hath forsaken me, having loved this present world. . . .
2 Timothy 4:10.

WE DO NOT know what lured Demas into deserting Paul. It may have been a girl, more money, the pleasures of sin, advancement toward earthly success. We know that today many a Demas, in the ministry and without, leaves Paul's standard, his theology, his pattern of life, what he stood for, his view of the future. And there may be a key to it in the very name *Demas*. *Demas* means popular, and popularity— the favor of this age—devastates many a life and many a church today. But if any man love the world, the love of the Father is not in him and whosoever will be a friend of this world is God's enemy. Our Lord made it clear for all time in John 15:18,19. Read it and make up your mind.

NOVEMBER 6

LOST

The Son of Man is come to seek and to save that which was lost.
Luke 19:10.

IT HAS BEEN a long time since I have heard parents speak of their unsaved boy or girl as being lost. That old word has departed from our Christian vocabulary. Young couples who are prospering materially and socially are admired and congratulated, but, if they do not know Jesus Christ, they are not doing well. We act as though their lostness were incidental, that it does not matter much, a personal and private matter not in good taste as a matter of discussion. Either it is a stupendous issue of heaven or hell or we might as well forget it. If our unsaved friends were in danger otherwise, we would go to their assistance without apology. Yet Jesus came to seek and to save the lost and died for their redemption. There is something hypocritical about claiming to believe that and acting as though it were unimportant.

NOVEMBER 7

TO GOD BE THE GLORY!

The Lord, he is the God; the Lord, he is the God.   1 Kings 18:39.

WHEN THE FIRE fell on Carmel, the people did not say, "Elijah, he is the great prophet!" but "The Lord, He is the God." God's purpose is not to show us strong in His behalf, but Himself strong in our behalf (2 Chronicles 16:9). Facing Goliath, David prayed that all men might know not that there was a David in the camp, but "that there is a God in Israel" (1 Samuel 17:46). Elijah's prayer on Carmel was that "this people may know that thou art the Lord God . . ." (1 Kings 18:37). When that is our objective, then the fire will fall and we shall see revival. We begin with, "Hallelujah, *Thine* the glory!" and end singing, "To God be the glory, great things He hath done."

NOVEMBER 8

AND A NEW EARTH

And I saw a new heaven and a new earth. . . .   Revelation 21:1.

IT IS OFTEN said that history begins in a garden and ends in a city. Humanity has moved to the city and America threatens to become one monstrous megalopolis from Maine to California. Revelation tells of two great cities at the end of time, Babylon and the New Jerusalem. But it also informs us that there will be a new earth. I am a country-man. I never saw a city I wanted to live in. I am an incurable rustic. I anticipate the Great White City that's soon coming down, but I thrill also at the prospect of a new earth with plenty of room to stroll in the countryside. There will be plenty of space for both urbanites and ruralists. Just what a new earth, free from all the distempers and pests and storms that beset us now, will be like I cannot comprehend now. But I am glad that along with the City there is also the Country. God will not let the devil get away with the havoc he wrought here. Paradise shall be restored.

NOVEMBER 9

PRESENT IN THE BODY

Whether present or absent. . . .   2 Corinthians 5:9.

THIS MORNING I enter another day in this old body on this old earth before Jesus comes or I go. That world of spirit awaits me where I shall await the resurrection and a new outfit unless my Lord comes before I die. Paul speaks of being absent from the body and present with the Lord. But being present in the body does not mean being absent from the Lord, for He lives in all who believe, and these bodies are the temples of the Holy Spirit. I am so glad we may know Him in these present bodies, know Him when, as spirits, we are present with Him and know Him eternally when that resurrection morning breaks. And I am glad that present in the body does not mean being absent from the Lord!

NOVEMBER 10

LILIES OF THE FIELD

Consider the lilies of the field. . . .   Matthew 6:28.

NOT ARTIFICIAL MAN-MADE lilies or protected lilies of the hothouse, but lilies of the open field exposed to wind and rain. They may not look as good, sometimes frayed and torn by tempest, too much sun or too much rain, bedraggled maybe, but real lilies. Some Christians who have wrestled long with the powers of darkness and suffered the pressures of this age may not be as elegant as manufactured varieties or sheltered souls who have not been in the thick of the fight. Paul was perhaps not an impressive sight physically. Some of the things he wrote indicate such limitations. Compared to some of the scribes in all their fancy garb, he looked like the itinerant battle-scarred veteran —this Gospel vagabond on the earth—that he was. The list he gives us of what he had been through (2 Corinthians 11:23–28) would make that abundantly clear. We need more lilies *of the field* out in the wind and weather.

NOVEMBER 11

POWER FOR THE PREDICAMENT

And now, Lord, behold their threatenings. . . . the place was shaken. . . .   Acts 4:29,31.

THE SPIRIT FELL in power to meet the crisis. God does not break through where nothing is going on. Whether Moses at the Red Sea, Gideon facing the Midianites, David meeting Goliath, the Hebrew children in the fiery furnace, the church in extremity, God comes

Oct 9   1/23/85
Nov 18   1/25/85
Sept. 10 2/1/85
July 7   2/18/85

March 14 2/22/85
Feb 27   2/27/85
March 28 4/15/85

when we are in trouble. He does not break through at Ichabod Memorial Church where nothing is happening. We have to stand at Carmel facing a showdown with Baal with the sacrifice drenched in water and create a situation so hopeless that, if God doesn't do something, we're sunk. When we undertake what is too much for *us,* God gets a chance!

NOVEMBER 12

TOO LATE TO CHANGE

He that is unjust, let him be unjust still: and he which is filthy, let him be filthy still: and he that is righteous, let him be righteous still: and he that is holy, let him be holy still.   Revelation 22:11.

CHARACTER TENDS TO congeal, to solidify as time goes on. The putty hardens into permanent form. We become fixed with time and fixed for eternity. Evil men grow worse and good men grow better and the day comes when it is too late to change. Moab settles on his lees and is no longer emptied from vessel to vessel. Someone has said, "No worse punishment can God give to unholy men than to give them up to themselves." Make much of the trend toward permanence if you are in God's way. Be fearful and check it with repentance and tears if your coldness toward God is solidifying. The day will come when he that is unjust and filthy will remain so for eternity.

NOVEMBER 13

LONELY MORNING

And God shall wipe away all tears from their eyes. . . .
Revelation 21:4.

TODAY I TRUDGED along in my loneliness, among strangers as usual and missed so much my companion of the years. But I found comfort in the familiar lines of Thomas Shephard:

How happy are the saints above,
Who once went sorrowing here!
But now they taste unmingled love
And joy without a tear.

I am glad for every dear one now with the Lord. We who still walk sorrowing here grow happy that soon He will come or we will go. The clock ticks out the few remaining hours before it becomes forever day!

NOVEMBER 14

SPECTATORS

And the people answered him not a word. . . . I Kings 18:21.
And sitting down they watched him there. . . . Matthew 27:36.

WHEN ELIJAH CALLED the priests of Baal and the people of Israel to a showdown between God and Baal, they refused to take a stand. At Calvary, they crucified my Lord and then they watched Him die. Whether Carmel or Calvary, we have set forth here that spectatoritis is the sin of both country and church today. We are a nation of onlookers, a grandstand generation in the stadium, at the show, at home watching television. The church has become a professional pulpitism financed by lay spectators. Everything is geared to showmanship and entertainment that involves no commitment. It is easier to dramatize than to duplicate so what was once an experience has become a performance. We are playactors which is of course another way of saying *hypocrites.*

NOVEMBER 15

SETTLED

It is finished. . . . John 19:30.

WHEN JESUS SAID, "It is finished," the issue was forever settled. God's Son became our sin. We do not settle *that* issue, but one thing we must settle: what we do about it. We Christians ought to get excited about it and remember that our business, whatever we do for a living, is to get the Gospel out. We act as though the fact were fiction. Everything has been done that can be done about the problem of sin. Jesus Christ is the Answer and, if the work is finished, there is nothing we can add to it. But there is an unfinished work of getting the message out. It was a great day for Hudson Taylor when he saw the finished work of Christ, but he spent the rest of his days in the unfinished work.

NOVEMBER 16

WHEN PRESSED BY MANY A FOE

The fiery darts of the wicked.   Ephesians 6:16.

BE NOT SURPRISED if doubts and fears assail you. They are to be expected like evil thoughts or disease germs. You cannot avoid being attacked and, if you are sore beset, remember that the Book has told you they will come. It is not wrong to be the target of their onslaughts, but you need not be overcome by them. It means that you are in real conflict and dangerous enough to the devil to bring on his hostility. If you wonder why they seem to increase as you go on and grow older, it is because the fight gets hotter as you grow in grace and it never lets up. But greater is He that is in you than all your adversaries. You are pressed by many a foe so that you may be all the more helpful to others who are not shadowboxing but are in the thick of the fight.

NOVEMBER 17

BELIEVE AND RECEIVE

Yet believing, ye rejoice . . . Receiving the end of your faith, even the salvation of your souls.   1 Peter 1:8,9.

THE FORMULA FOR all the blessings of God is *believe* and *receive*. To all who believe, power is given to become sons of God—even to them that believe on His Name (John 1:12). When we pray, if we believe that we receive, we shall have what we ask (Mark 11:24). Our Lord spoke of the Spirit which they that believe on Him should receive (John 7:39). We believe God's Word, we receive His Son and with Him all things freely given in Him (Romans 8:32). We see Him not, yet believing, we rejoice. Believe, receive, believe you have received . . . and rejoice!

NOVEMBER 18

WIND AND WAVES

What manner of man is this, that even the winds and the sea obey him! Matthew 8:27.

MAN HAS NEVER had dominion over the wind and the sea. He uses them, but he cannot control them. The weather is unpredictable, often without rhyme or reason. Hurricanes and tidal waves with their attendant destruction and death were not part of God's original design. Weather is the despair of the meteorologist and the forecaster. Man was given dominion over the creatures of land, sea, and air, but the wind and the waves were beyond his jurisdiction from the outset. Recently a fine Bible teacher said: "Then Jesus came and stilled the storm and His disciples cried, 'What manner of man is this that the WINDS and the SEA obey Him!' "

NOVEMBER 19

BUT HIM THEY SAW NOT

But him they saw not. Luke 24:24.

THE DISCIPLES WENT to the sepulchre, found the grave empty, the linen graveclothes, but they did not see the risen Lord. We may believe in the Resurrection, see the evidences, accept the facts without living contact with the One who rose. We may argue for the event, build up a case for the doctrine, but never see by living faith the One it is all about. That makes us apologists but not apostles. The flaming witness does not say, "I saw the grave, I believe the evidence." The apostle says, "I saw the Lord!"

NOVEMBER 20

IN THE BREAKING OF BREAD

And they told what things were done in the way, and how he was known of them in breaking of bread.   Luke 24:35.

THE EMMAUS MEAL was not a miracle meal like the feeding of the five thousand nor a special meal like the Last Supper. Yet it was both because the risen Lord was there! It is in simplest things that our living Lord is revealed. When He simply said, "Mary." When He told the fisherman disciples, "Cast the net on the right side." When He broke bread. It was so like the Master! And dear Alexander Whyte thinks the Emmaus disciples really knew Him when they saw the print of the nails in His hands!

NOVEMBER 21

LAWYER IN THE HALL

Behold, the judge standeth before the door.   James 5:9. *We have an advocate with the Father. . . .*   1 John 2:1.

A MAN ON trial was informed by the judge that he could choose a lawyer. "There is one on your right, one on your left, and there is another out in the hall." The man on trial looked to the right and left and said, "Judge, I'll take a chance on the man in the hall." The Christian is not interested in the right and left wings since, as one of our fine preachers says, they are both flapping on the same old bird. The Christian has a Lawyer out in the hall, an Advocate in the wings, at the door, soon to return. And our Advocate is also the Judge!

NOVEMBER 22

NOT TIME YET

Mine hour is not yet come.   John 2:4.

OUR LORD CAME first to the lost sheep of Israel. He came also to die for our sins and to rise for our justification. One day He will return to reign. Have you wondered why He healed only a comparative few on His first visit? That was not His main business then. But He healed some, raised a few from the dead, did many wonders as an advance demonstration of how it will be when He comes to set up the visible Kingdom. The miracles were an earnest, a foretaste of the powers of the age to come. We must understand what He did in the light of when and why He did it. How this first taste whets our appetites for the steady fare which shall be ours when He comes again!

NOVEMBER 23

THE COSTLY OFFERING

And the water ran round about the altar. . . .   I Kings 18:35.

AFTER THREE AND a half years of drought with no rain on the just or unjust, water must have been the scarcest thing in Israel. Yet Elijah poured twelve barrels of it on the Carmel sacrifice. When we pray for fire from heaven, we must offer the most precious thing we have on the repaired and prepared altar. It was as though Elijah poured out freely that which was so scarce, expecting God to answer with abundance of rain. Give God the best, what is most rare and precious, like water in time of drought.

NOVEMBER 24

SWEAT

His sweat was as it were great drops of blood falling down to the ground. Luke 22:44.

BECAUSE OF HIS disobedience, Adam was sentenced to earn his bread by the sweat of his face (Genesis 3:19). We are still under that sentence although we have devised clever ways to avoid sweating it out. Our Lord sweated blood in the agony of the Garden as He faced His death for our sins. Ezekiel saw a vision of the future temple and its priests, who would wear nothing that caused sweat—for nothing of fleshly effort could enter into that service (Ezekiel 44:18). They that are in the flesh cannot please God. Our Lord sweated blood to pay the penalty of Adam's sin and to bring us to that good day when nothing of old Adam shall enter into the temple of the coming Kingdom.

NOVEMBER 25

NO TRIP TO PARADISE

And lest I should be exalted above measure. . . .
2 Corinthians 12:7.

SOME OF US have wished we might have rare supernatural experiences like some we read about. But we can serve our generation better and relate to the rank and file of humanity if we have known no angel visitant, no opening skies but rather a simple daily walk with God. We might be exalted above measure and take pride in relating our trip to Third Heaven and others might feel that we were too far ahead of them to be of help in their plodding lives. It is better not to have such rare revelations if we can minister better to others who have had no "trip to Paradise."

NOVEMBER 26

MESSENGER OR SATAN

There was given to me a thorn in the flesh, the messenger of Satan to buffet me. . . . 2 Corinthians 12:7.

IT MIGHT HAVE been embarrassing to Paul, who had been used to heal others, that he must carry a thorn in his flesh that God would not remove. He had healed others, but himself he could not heal. God works in strange ways to make us spiritually strong when we are weak, by making us physically weak when we were strong. We are not to groan about it but rather glory in it—not glorify our infirmities but glory *in* them, and take pleasure in them if by them the power of Christ may rest upon us. Moreover, we recognize the scourge for what it is—a messenger of Satan allowed in God's permissive will.

NOVEMBER 27

FIGHTINGS AND FEARS

Without were fightings, within were fears. 2 Corinthians 7:5.

THE CHRISTIAN WHO has been a long time on the road may be troubled when he discovers that doubts and fears increase instead of subsiding into a tranquil calm as he nears home. To the contrary, they may increase and intensify. This world is not our rest. There is reason to suspect some dear souls who think they have reached a haven ahead of time and who say they are no longer beset by the powers of evil. Paul wrestled with the powers of darkness to the finish and had no idyllic old age in a favored spot. The reward is not in the absence of the enemy but in the presence of the Lord with us, the Fourth in the Fiery Furnace.

NOVEMBER 28

REJOICING IN INIQUITY

[Charity] rejoiceth not in iniquity, but rejoiceth in the truth. . . .
1 Corinthians 13:6.

THIS HAS BEEN translated, "Love does not gloat over wickedness," and "Love does not rejoice at wrong." Men love darkness rather than light because their deeds are evil. This explains why muckraking and mudslinging books about the sins of good men are more popular than biographies of the saints. The heart is deceitful and desperately wicked, and evil is the natural bent of man. The field left idle returns to weeds and thorns. The public likes to read the confessions of national figures who get into trouble. Read the news media and see what the readers want. Sin cleans up on the newsstands and virtue is uninteresting. But the Christian sets himself against the tide and rejoices in the annals of men and women who walk with God.

NOVEMBER 29

NOT LOOKING FOR MIRACLES

All things continue as they were from the beginning of the creation.
2 Peter 3:4.

ONE PROBLEM NOW is that we have a Bible full of miracles, but today we live in a world of cause and effect with few breakthroughs from heaven. How to believe the one and live in the other perplexes not a few. For the most part, the church "insists on the Lord's providences being draped in the habiliments of decent cause and effect, and attired in the surplice of natural law and order lest God should make bare His holy arm in the eyes of all the nations." So wrote A. J. Gordon and the situation has degenerated more since then. God does not perform His wonders in an unbelieving church that does not expect them.

NOVEMBER 30

TO SEEM OR TO BE

Thou hast a name that thou livest, and art dead. . . .
Revelation 3:1.

THE OLD MOTTO *Esse quam videri* (To be rather than to seem) needs
to be reactivated in these times. A prominent minister said, "The more
we seem to be what we are not, the smaller our chance of becoming
what we might be." The church at Sardis had a name to be alive, not
to be dead, and, if it had such a reputation, there must have been a
lot of activity to build up and maintain that illusion. But it kept them
so busy that they never had time to become what they might have
been. The Pharisees spent their time *seeming,* they were playactors,
hypocrites, phonies. *Seeming* involves more than just striking a pose.
It takes dedication and hard work to be a successful poseur! And it
keeps us from becoming what we might have been.

DECEMBER 1

WHOSE PRISONER ARE YOU?

Paul, a prisoner of Jesus Christ. . . .   Philemon 1;
see Ephesians 3:1;4:1.

PAUL WAS NOT the prisoner of himself—shut up to what he wanted
to be or do—for he stood in the liberty wherewith Christ had set him
free. He was not the prisoner of circumstances. He was not the prisoner of a parish, a church flunkey, for he was a pastor to all the
churches. He was not imprisoned by a sect, confined within any *ism.*
He had belonged to "the most straitest sect . . . a Pharisee" (Acts
26:5), and he belonged to "the way which they call heresy" (Acts
24:14), but his was the liberty of the Gospel. He was not a prisoner
of Rome, nor of Caesar, but of Jesus Christ, Master of all conditions
within and without.

DECEMBER 2

MAKE IT CONTEMPORARY!

Christ died for our sins . . . was buried . . . and rose again. . . .
1 Corinthians 15:3,4. *I will come again. . . .* John 14:3.

EVERY CHRISTIAN SHOULD live as though Jesus died yesterday. In his heart and thoughts he should keep Calvary up-to-date. His song should be, "Near the cross! O Lamb of God, Bring its scenes before me; Help me walk from day to day with its shadows o'er me." He should live as though Jesus rose this morning, for every morning is a resurrection day. We ought to greet each sunrise with the shout, "He's alive!" And every Christian ought to live as though Jesus might come tonight. He could come anytime, but it will be as a thief in the night. We believe all this, but sometimes it is only past history or future hope. Make it contemporary!

DECEMBER 3

COLD CREAM ON CANCER

For they have healed the hurt of the daughter of my people slightly, saying, Peace, peace; when there is no peace. Jeremiah 8:11.

IT IS A grievous matter to tone down and treat lightly the sins of this generation or evils in the church. It is cold cream on cancer, a Band-Aid on a blood clot. Our Lord called for major surgery on the offending eye or hand. Paul did not cheerfully dismiss the evils in Corinth by saying that things could be worse. Our Lord dealt seriously with the churches of Asia. We are not called to look on the bright side but on the right side and sometimes the right side gets darker before it gets brighter. We do a great disfavor to an ailing country or church to cry, "Peace" when there is no peace. We dishonor God and contribute to the worsening of the situation. We are not to be pessimistic or optimistic but realistic.

DECEMBER 4

LAVERS FROM LOOKING GLASSES

And he made the laver of brass, and the foot of it of brass, of the lookingglasses of the women assembling, which assembled at the door of the tabernacle of the congregation.   Exodus 38:8.

THE LAVER FOR cleansing was made from the mirrors donated by the women. Thus the symbols of pride and vanity were surrendered to be melted into a vessel of the Lord. God's spiritual temple is furnished with the yielded emblems of our egotism and self-glory refined in the fires of repentance. Our looking glasses must become lavers. The earrings of the Israelites were fashioned by Aaron into a golden calf and by Gideon into an ephod that became an idol. Our trinkets become either idols or lavers depending on those who offer them either to the deification of our pride or to its destruction.

DECEMBER 5

WHEN EVERYTHING IS NEW

Behold, I make all things new.   Revelation 21:5.

TO LAY AWAY the form of a dear one, once lovely but now disfigured, mind disturbed, personality changed, is a soul-jarring experience. It is sad enough when one goes in possession of faculties, fully conscious, wearing a smile. But Satan need not rejoice for he has not had the last laugh. God will make all things new, including a new mind and body for my beloved and a personality refined and glorified and yet, I believe, enough like her former self to be recognizable as was our Lord in His new form. I am not singing in the dark nor whistling past the graveyard. It is guaranteed by both the written and living Word. I can hardly wait to see it happen!

DECEMBER 6

MORE THAN A TEACHER

No man cometh unto the Father, but by me.   John 14:6.

THOSE SUAVE INTELLECTUALS and all other unbelievers who see in Jesus Christ only a man and only a teacher overlook one stupendous fact: there is a built-in contradiction. If Jesus were only a teacher, even if He were the greatest teacher and the greatest man, He was either a lunatic or an impostor because He claimed to be far more. We must either consider Him a fraud or kneel before Him as the Son of God. He did not come as a great and merely human teacher and He does not want our congratulations; He does not ask compliments but commitment, absolute surrender to Him as Saviour and Lord. The highest tribute we can pay to Him as only a man is an insult. "All things are delivered unto me of my Father: and no man knoweth the Son, but the Father; neither knoweth any man the Father, save the Son, and he to whomsoever the Son will reveal him" (Matthew 11:27; *see* Luke 10:22). No human teacher can say that.

DECEMBER 7

THE HOPE-FULL OUTLOOK

Looking for that blessed hope. . . .   Titus 2:13.

IF YOU ARE going by the news broadcasts and the "world situation," the outlook today is hopeless. The human race has painted itself into a corner and all the experts are at wit's end. The pointers-with-pride have been superseded by the viewers-with-alarm. But the Christian, who is looking for the glorious appearance of the great God and our Saviour Jesus Christ, has the hopeful outlook because his is the Blessed Hope. He is hopeful because he is Hope full! He does not sorrow as those who have no hope and, having this hope in him, he purifies himself. It is a hope-full outlook because it is a hope-full uplook. Keep looking up!

DECEMBER 8

WATERS THAT FAIL?

He will not fail thee. . . .   Deuteronomy 31:6,8; *see* Joshua 1:5;
1 Chronicles 28:20.

MY LITTLE RADIO on my desk is tuned into a Christian broadcasting station. Any time and all the time, I can hear prayers and sermons and songs of the faith. They are the accumulated testimony of the centuries and nothing can make me believe that all these longings of millions through history for God, for salvation, for healing, for guidance, for comfort, for a heaven to come, for reunion with dear ones lost a while—nobody can make me even suspect that all this will be as a cup held to the lips only to be dashed to the ground. In his lowest moments, Jeremiah may mourn, "Wilt thou be unto me as waters that fail?" but history bears abundant answer that God's compassions fail not, that He did not, cannot, will not fail. He abideth faithful. I believe it. It pillows my head at night and lifts it up by day.

DECEMBER 9

TURNING THE TABLES

All power is given unto me. . . . *Go ye therefore* . . . *I am with
you.* . . .   Matthew 28:18–20.

THE GREAT COMMISSION does not sound like a call to defensive warfare. The Church is not a beleaguered garrison whose business is just to hold out until Jesus comes. True, the world will not be converted, but it can be confronted with a victorious faith. We have forgotten that we are apostles more than apologists and *apologetic* has taken on the meaning of merely defending what we believe instead of marching into offensive warfare with our Waterloo behind us, won by our Captain on Calvary and the open grave. Let us turn the tables on the enemy like the old captain who shouted when informed that his company was surrounded by the foe, "Don't let one of them escape!"

DECEMBER 10

THE ANSWERS ARE IN THE BACK!

Write the things which thou hast seen, and the things which are, and the things which shall be hereafter. . . . Revelation 1:19.

WHEN I WAS a boy in school, my record in arithmetic was deplorable. But I always remembered that the answers were all in the back of the book! In my Bible, there are many things I do not understand and "the things which are" puzzle me these days. But this little Book of Revelation tells me not only about that, but also that which is to be. If we know where we are going, we are better prepared for where we are today. This little book closes with the victory of Christ, the new heaven and earth and all things made new. I read in the papers what man is doing, but I read in this little book what God is going to do. I may not fully comprehend all I read, but I get the message. The answers are all there and they are good!

DECEMBER 11

NOT WHAT BUT WHOM

For I know whom I have believed. . . . 2 Timothy 1:12.

THE FAMILIAR THREE-POINTER—Fact, Faith, Feeling—is useful in simplifying the correct order of Christian faith, but, strictly speaking, we are not saved by faith in any one of these. It is possible to believe the historic facts about Jesus Christ without personally trusting Him. It is possible to have faith in our faith without trusting Him. It is not our faith, but the Faithful One that matters most. We may trust our feelings and that is the weakest crutch of all, for feelings rise and fall like a thermometer in the spring. We must accept the facts about our Lord, we must trust Him, and the feelings will follow, but the heart of it all is not *what* but *Whom*.

DECEMBER 12

COSMETICS

That women adorn themselves in modest apparel.... 1 Timothy
2:9. *Whose adorning let it not be that outward adorning ... But
let it be the hidden man of the heart....* 1 Peter 3:3,4.

WALK THROUGH THE cosmetic section of any great department store
and your imagination is overwhelmed at the fabulous magnitude of
the empire of cosmetics alone. You think of *kosmos,* the earth, the
world order, the people on the earth, then the further meanings of the
word in *arrangement, adornment* and you wind up with *cosmetics.* A
sensible and judicious use of some of it may not be amiss (we see many
who could profit from a little!), but when you compare the time,
energy, and billions of dollars spent in prettying up the natural man
(and such poor results!) with the slovenly state of our inner souls, the
admonitions of Paul and Peter, old-fashioned as they sound, ought to
convict us of what creatures of the cosmos even we Christians are
today. It's about time churches opened up beauty shops for the soul!

DECEMBER 13

THE TENT AND THE BUILDING

*For we know that if our earthly house of this tabernacle were
dissolved, we have a building of God, an house not made with
hands, eternal in the heavens.* 2 Corinthians 5:1.

I AWAKE EACH morning to find myself still in this old body in this
old world. But shortly I put off this old tent and then await my new
home, my new resurrection body. Paul longed for that new garment,
his "Easter outfit." He does not have the resurrection body yet and
there is much about the intermediate state of the spirits now absent
from the body and present with the Lord that we do not understand,
but the soul does not sleep. Paul was not anticipating sleep, but to be
with Christ which is far better.

DECEMBER 14

SEPARATION AND INVOLVEMENT

In the world. . . . not of the world.   John 17:11,14.

THE CHRISTIAN HAS been saved out of the world. He is in the world but not of it and he is sent into the world to win others out of the world, which is his business in this world. He must keep separated from its defilements, yet he must be in the midst of it for the salt must be mixed with whatever it is to purify. Light is needed in a dark place, not in a light place. We are to be separated from all that might hinder our witness, but we are to separate from sin and not from sinners. The Pharisees would not even eat an egg that had been laid on the Sabbath, but they wrapped the robes of their supersanctity around them and would not touch poor sinners with a forty-foot pole. How to be a separated mixer, both apart and involved, is a lesson learned in the school of our Lord who was both.

DECEMBER 15

THE PRACTICE OF THE ABSENCE OF GOD

There is no fear of God before their eyes.   Romans 3:18.

WE ARE FAMILIAR with Brother Lawrence and his *Practice of the Presence of God,* but someone has called *secularism* the Practice of His Absence. It is the way of life for this generation. To moderns for the most part, this universe is a machine wound up and running down with no purpose behind it, no objective before it. We live as though God did not exist, as though man were the arbiter of his own destiny. At most He is dismissed as a grandfather trotting his children on his knee and winking at the wickedness of the sons of men. We have made our own noose and the stage is set for the hanging of civilization. The issue remains: Is God nowhere or is He now here?

DECEMBER 16

NO OTHER GODS

Thou shalt have no other gods before me. Exodus 20:3.

OUR LORD MADE it clear that all other loves must be as hate compared to our love for Him (*see* Luke 14:26). This does not mean we love dear ones less, but that we love Him more. We must not water down this word until it loses its meaning. A departed dear one can become an idol at whose shrine we worship—so can our work, our reputation, our pleasures, some human friendship, our possessions. We must live *as though* these did not exist, so far as our supreme love and loyalty are concerned. When anything else eclipses our devotion to Jesus Christ, it must go and sometimes God takes it. He will not share the throne room of our hearts with anyone or anything else. But when He is first and last, all other legitimate and proper interests and affections find their places. But they must never hold the status of gods or idols.

DECEMBER 17

THE DIVINE DESIGN

But he [chastens us] for our profit. . . . Hebrews 12:10.

THE FLAME SHALL not hurt thee—I only design
Thy dross to consume and thy gold to refine.

SOMETIMES GOD CHASTENS us and sometimes Satan sifts us. God's purpose is to burn up the dross and refine the gold. Satan hopes to winnow out the wheat and leave only the chaff, but God can turn it around the other way. At any rate, our Father takes no pleasure in our sorrows and grief. His only design is to refine us. Alas, there is often so much dross and so little gold, so much chaff and so little wheat, so much wood, hay, and stubble, so little gold, silver, and precious stones! We may not have much left when He is finished with us, but a little gold is better than tons of chaff. It is a good day when we give up trash for treasure.

DECEMBER 18

RALLY IN THE LAST INNING

Thy youth is renewed like the eagle's.   Psalms 103:5.

SOMETIMES A BALL team that has played poorly most of the game takes a spurt and rallies to win in the last inning. Old age besets us in time, our heart and strength fail us, and it is hard to know whether we are suffering from hardening of the arteries or hardening of the "hearteries." The text tells us that our youth may be renewed as the eagle's and the last chapter may be the best. It is not always so, but it happens often enough to encourage us for a rally in the last inning. You never can tell when God will do it and we do well to prepare for the possibility even if it is not a probability!

DECEMBER 19

WE STILL HAVE JESUS

But now we see not yet all things put under him. But we see Jesus. . . .   Hebrews 2:8,9.

JEREMIAH CATALOGS THE miseries of his day but ends, "Thou, O Lord, remainest for ever . . ." (Lamentations 5:19). Micah does the same, saying, "Therefore I will look unto the Lord . . ." (7:7). And again Hebrews speaks of God's creative works saying, "They shall perish; but thou remainest . . ." (1:11). We certainly do not see all things put under our Lord, but we see Him and He is the guarantee of a better day. There is so much that we do not see, but we see Him. And what we do see must be judged and valued in the light of Him.

DECEMBER 20

MORE BEYOND!

Thou art old and stricken in years, and there remaineth yet very much land to be possessed. Joshua 13:1.

MIND YOU, GOD did not say to this veteran, "You are getting old and you've had it"! On the Pillars of Hercules was a warning to sailors, *Ne plus ultra,* which means "no more beyond." That was the limit beyond which mariners dared not venture. But Joaquin Miller in his immortal poem about Columbus began,

> Behind him lay the gray Azores,
> Behind the Gates of Hercules.

That was really a starting point for Columbus. He believed there was more beyond and we Americans are living on that *more* today! For the Christian, there lies far more to be possessed here and now and beyond that, new heavens and earth! God grant the Church today some hardy souls who, while frightened or complacent saints rebel, know only one reply, "Sail on! sail on! and *on!*" And of such it shall be said, "He gained a world: he gave the Church its grandest lesson: On! sail on!"

DECEMBER 21

WE NEED A LIFT!

Looking unto Jesus. . . . Hebrews 12:2.

WE NEED TO lift up our eyes, our heads, our hands, our voices. All is commanded in the Scriptures. There are too many downcast disciples, eyes down; too many defeated saints, heads drooped; too many with hands not lifted in worship; too many silent saints who need to cry aloud and spare not, lifting their voices like a trumpet. We need a great uplifting!

DECEMBER 22

THE UNSEEN CAPTAIN

As captain of the host of the Lord am I now come.   Joshua 5:14.

WITH JORDAN BEHIND him and Jericho before him, Joshua was no doubt pondering the seriousness of his situation when he met his heavenly ally against the host of his adversaries. I remember a great sermon by Dr. Paul Rees based on this meeting and it had three points: There was a *heritage* to be received, a *hindrance* to be removed, and a *Helper* to be recognized. We tend to count our adversaries and forget our unseen allies. Remember the horses and chariots around Elisha, and our Lord in the Garden saying to Peter, "I could call down more than twelve legions of angels" (*see* Matthew 26:53). We are before Jericho today and we need a fresh meeting with the Captain of the Lord of Hosts. There be many adversaries but there are more that be with us than they that be with them.

DECEMBER 23

TARGET OF SATAN

He that departeth from evil maketh himself a prey. . . .
Isaiah 59:15.

ANY MAN WHO takes Jesus Christ seriously becomes the target of the devil. Most church members do not give Satan enough trouble to arouse his opposition. This text has been translated, "Anyone who tries a better life is soon attacked" and "He that departeth from evil is accounted mad." The world's black sheep do not like white sheep for they show up the contrast. And nothing makes black sheep more comfortable that *dirty* white sheep! But actually, as our Lord said, we are sheep among wolves. That makes the contrast all the more marked and the opposition still worse.

DECEMBER 24

WHEREFORE DIDST THOU DOUBT?

Neither be ye of doubtful mind. Luke 12:29.

WE ARE TO believe without doubting (Matthew 21:21), pray without doubting (1 Timothy 2:8), obey without doubting (Acts 11:12). So much of our faith, our praying, our obedience, comes to naught because it is clogged with doubt, diluted with unbelief. Doubt puts the brakes on, takes all the assurance out of our hearts, makes us wavering disciples, driven by the wind and tossed. When our Lord appeared after His Resurrection, some believed but some doubted and one feels that chill in many a gathering of Christians. In questionable matters, "he that doubteth is condemned if he eat" and the underground principle is "whatsoever is not of faith is sin" (Romans 14:23). We believe or we doubt and if both be mixed let us earnestly pray, "Lord, I believe; help thou mine unbelief" (Mark 9:24). To the extent we are believing, we are not doubting and, if we are doubting, to that extent we are not believing. Beware of a doubtful mind.

DECEMBER 25

THE PATTERN OF BETHLEHEM

And she brought forth her firstborn son, and wrapped him in swaddling clothes, and laid him in a manger; because there was no room for them in the inn. Luke 2:7.

AT CHRISTMAS WE say much of the meaning of His coming to earth, the mission, the message, but we sometimes overlook the manner of His Advent. God set it up in a pattern we never would have dreamed. He was born in a stable to a lowly peasant couple in an insignificant town in an obscure corner of the Roman Empire. Think how we would have arranged it in this publicity-mad day! That same pattern my Lord followed all His days and the Church might take a hint today, when Hollywood sets the style.

DECEMBER 26

DAY AFTER CHRISTMAS

Jesus Christ the same yesterday, and today, and for ever.
Hebrews 13:8.

THE DAY AFTER Christmas is a day of broken toys, opened boxes, torn packages, thread and ribbons galore, the surprises all over, *thank you*s all said. A long time coming and so soon gone! But, when Jesus Christ is born in our hearts, there are no sad days after, no waiting a year, no putting away the *thank you*s for another twelve months. Every day is Christmas when the Saviour lives within, the same today as yesterday. Each day brings fresh gifts from above, not a holiday but a holy day. And we are not merely the recipients, we give because He gave, we love because He loved, and we want to share Him with everybody. Once-a-year Christmas on the calendar is precious, but there is no "day after" when we can say, "Christ liveth in me."

DECEMBER 27

NEW YEAR AHEAD!

I am with you alway. . . . Matthew 28:20.

THE TWINGE OF sadness when Christmas passes is relieved by the prospect of New Year next week. There is the excitement of a new beginning no matter what it may bring. But Christmas in the heart, through the indwelling Christ, brings not only a new year that starts immediately, but a new life that never ends. We don't wait a week to begin; eternal life does not start at death but now. We have it now as surely as we will ever have it, although the hereafter will bring fresh glories beyond our comprehension. For the Christian, there is not only a New Year on the calendar but a New Forever in the heart!

DECEMBER 28

NEVERTHELESS

Nevertheless the foundation of God standeth sure. . . .
2 Timothy 2:19.

YOU HAVE ONLY to check your Bible concordance to discover how often that word *nevertheless* shows up. Often against the dark background of conditions in this word, it turns the picture to say, "Notwithstanding, however, still, on the other hand, there is another side. . . ." In our text, Paul is writing to Timothy about false teachers, and, against their errors, he says God's foundation stands sure. He makes two observations: God knows them that are His, but His children are not to settle in complacency because of that security but rather depart from iniquity. Our blessed assurance is no excuse for careless living.

DECEMBER 29

THE "NEVERTHELESS" THAT MAKES THE DIFFERENCE

Master, we have toiled all the night, and have taken nothing: nevertheless at thy word I will let down the net. Luke 5:5.

AFTER A NIGHT of failure came the turn when they passed from defeat to victory, and they did it when they crossed the bridge marked *Nevertheless.* "We have toiled," Peter said, but now "at thy word, I will let down the net." When we move from *we* to *Thy,* we have crossed the bridge. After they caught a superabundance of fish, Jesus said, "Fear not; from henceforth thou shalt catch men" (5:10). When we cross the bridge called Nevertheless, the next sign reads HENCEFORTH. This is success.

DECEMBER 30

THE JUDGE ON TRIAL

Hereafter shall ye see the Son of man sitting on the right hand of power, and coming in the clouds of heaven. Matthew 26:64.

HERE ANOTHER *nevertheless* turns the tables. Our Lord is on trial, but He declares, "Nevertheless . . . this scene will change one day. I will be the Judge and you will be on trial." It was this affirmation of His return that opened the floodgates of wrath so that even the high priest rent his clothes. Jesus Christ is no longer on trial awaiting our verdict. We are awaiting His verdict! The prospect of that Great Assize throws even organized religion into a fit, rending their garments sometimes as it did here, but the Christian welcomes the day when the trial will be reversed by the Judge who will rend not His clothes but the clouds of heaven!

DECEMBER 31

SOMETHING NEW TOMORROW!

Nevertheless we, according to his promise, look for new heavens and a new earth, wherein dwelleth righteousness. 2 Peter 3:13.

THE YEAR ENDS with a world in turmoil, sudden destruction possible. Peter tells us of a coming catastrophe that sounds like an atomic holocaust. How up-to-date, ". . . the elements shall melt with fervent heat . . ." (3:10)! But the Christian is looking tonight not just for a new year but a new age—new heavens and earth where righteousness dwells. "Seeing then that all these things shall be dissolved, what manner of persons ought ye to be. . . . diligent that ye may be found of him in peace, without spot, and blameless" (3:11,14). While the world drinks and dances into the New Year to spend tomorrow with a hangover, let the Christian meet it on his knees and meet tomorrow with a hallelujah!